Pitch Black Heart Syndrome

Pitch Black Heart Syndrome

[**p**oems *and* **pictures**]

Written, photographed
and designed by

J. Scott Robinson

Cover art/design and interior formatting/design: J. Scott Robinson

www.jsrobinson.myportfolio.com

First Edition | Paperback
ISBN: 978-1-0689311-2-3

For you...

*In times of sadness and anger, and unsuccessfully
dodging the dangers of self-diagnosis, and losing
oneself to the darkness...*

*When you can't find the words, may you see your
own anguish reflected here, vomited forth from the
cold abyss that is the pitch black heart...*

*And though catharsis is temporary, may your pain
be validated and sedated...*

For you...

May you be okay, today and every day...

CONTENTS

Part I: Dirty Feathers

Part I: Dirty Feathers

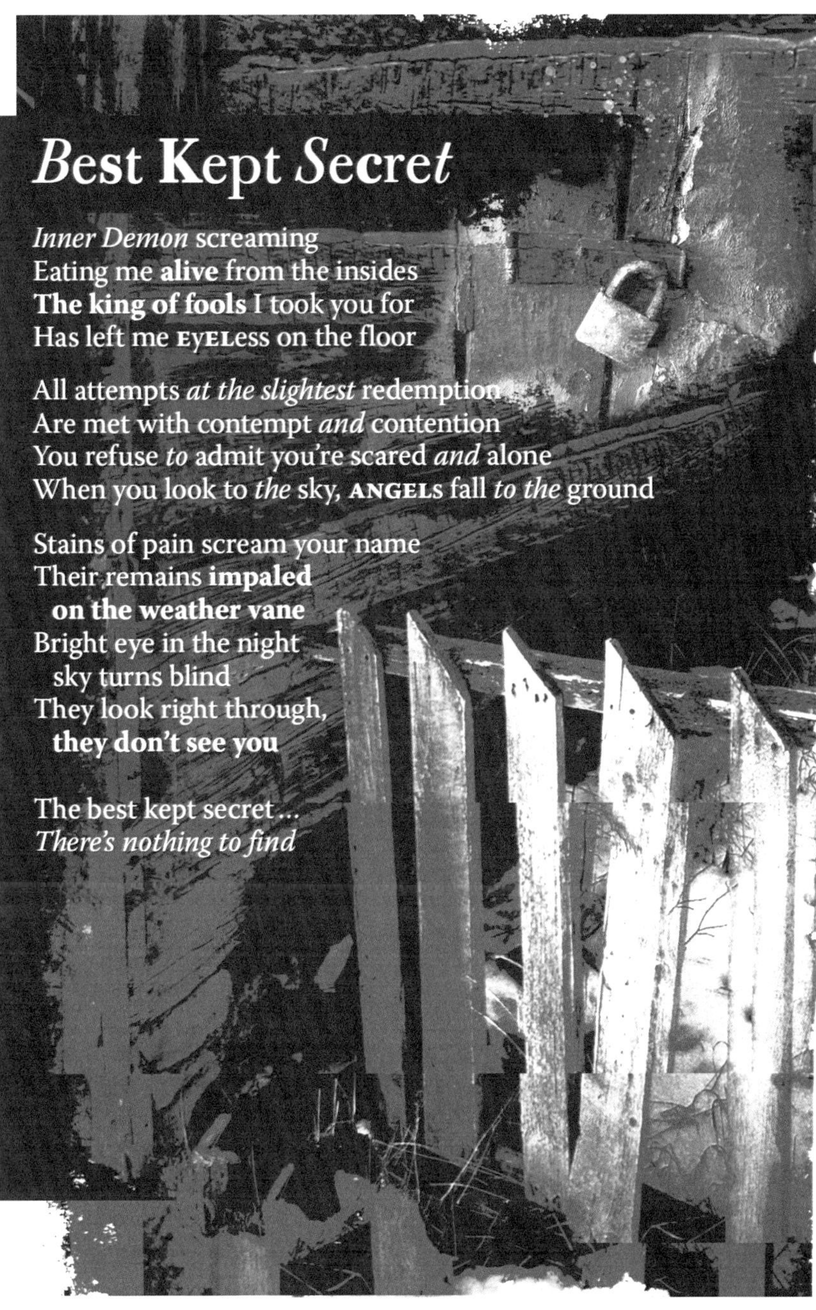

Best Kept Secret

Inner Demon screaming
Eating me **alive** from the insides
The king of fools I took you for
Has left me EYELESS on the floor

All attempts *at the slightest* redemption
Are met with contempt *and* contention
You refuse *to* admit you're scared *and* alone
When you look to *the* sky, ANGELS fall *to the* ground

Stains of pain scream your name
Their remains **impaled
on the weather vane**
Bright eye in the night
sky turns blind
They look right through,
they don't see you

The best kept secret…
There's nothing to find

Die Every Day

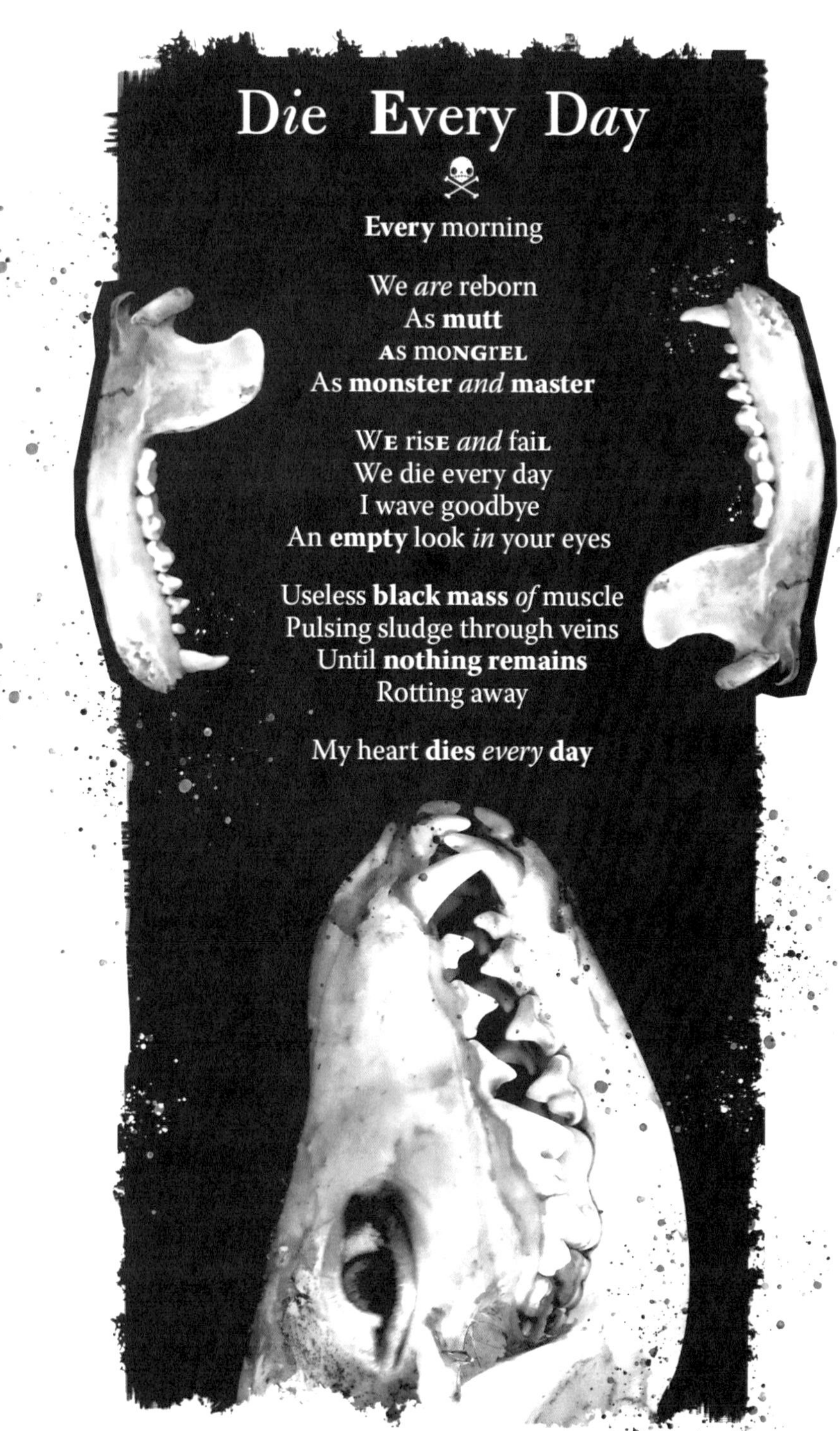

Lost *and* Too Far Gone

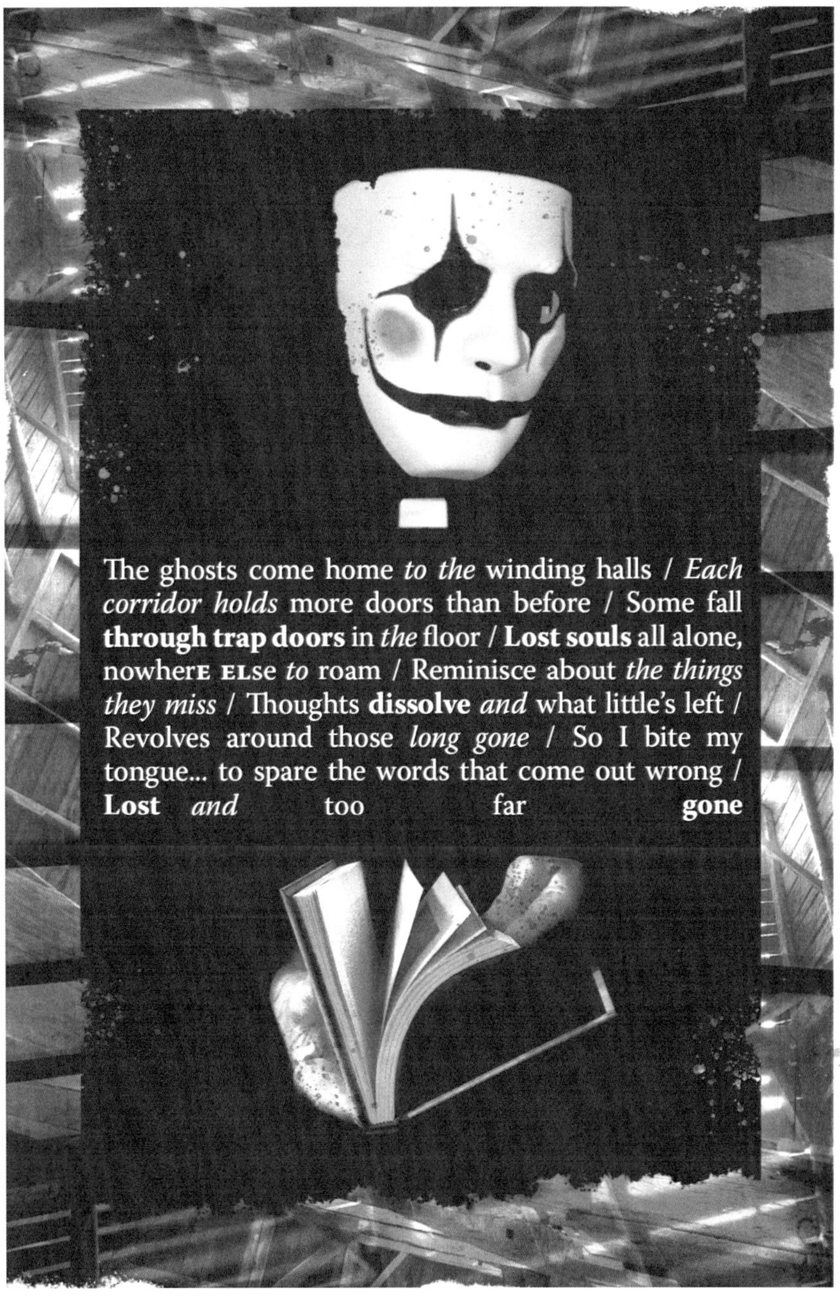

Idle Hands

My guardian ANGEL *fell to* **hell**

This darkness swells like *it* always does
I'm not **the man I thought** I was

Hear me, *fear* me
Say my name and **I'll appear before thee**

These idle hands
On your throat they land
Forced *to* knEEL
You struggle *to* stand

So **say goodbye** with tears *in your eyes*
You won't survive *or be* revived
What I can no longer hide *is the* **devil inside**

Scream *in* pain
Now **scream** *in* vain

Skin *you*
Burn *you*
Bury *you*

Alive

Artificial Sentiment

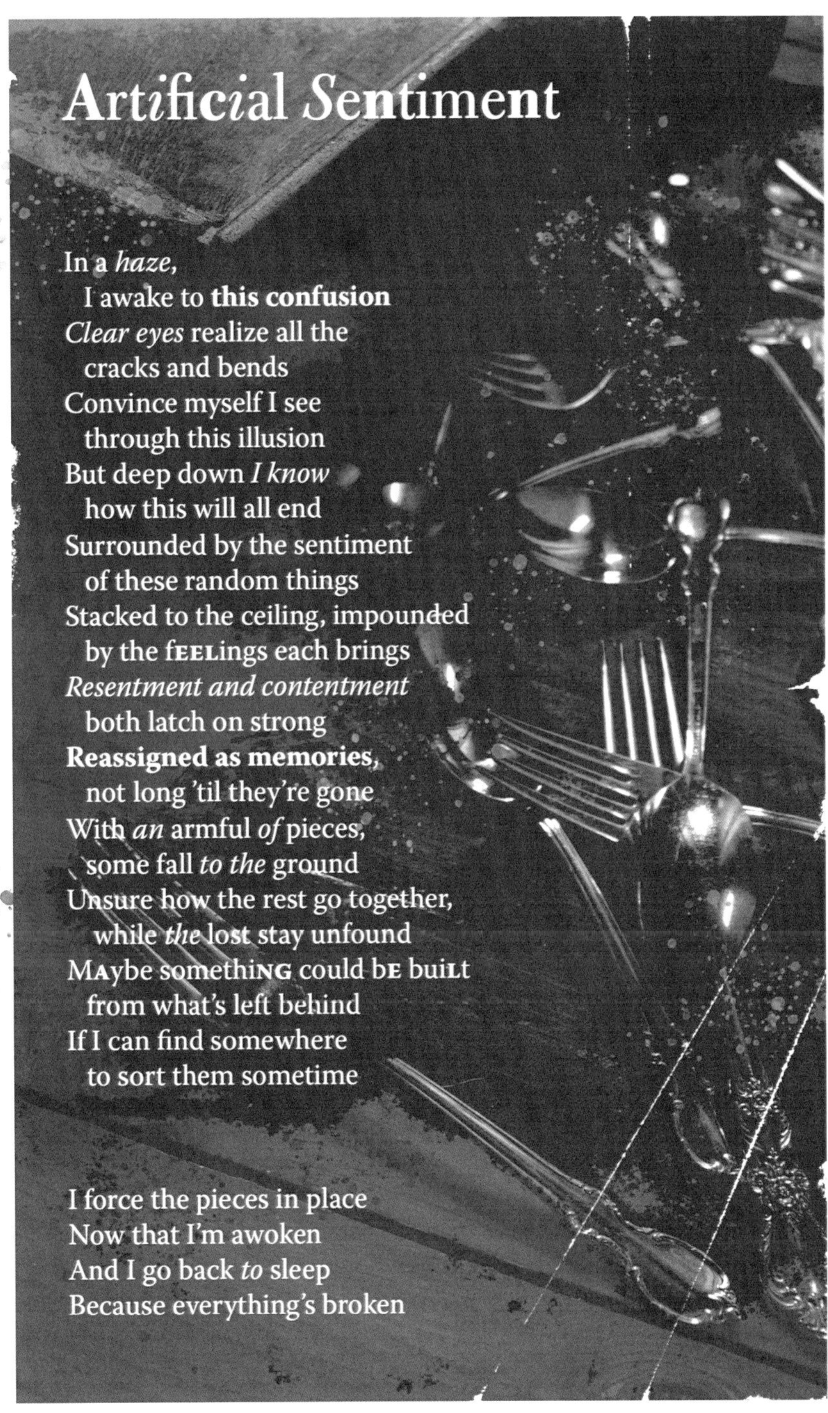

In a *haze*,
  I awake to **this confusion**
Clear eyes realize all the
  cracks and bends
Convince myself I see
  through this illusion
But deep down *I know*
  how this will all end
Surrounded by the sentiment
  of these random things
Stacked to the ceiling, impounded
  by the feelings each brings
Resentment and contentment
  both latch on strong
Reassigned as memories,
  not long 'til they're gone
With *an* armful *of* pieces,
  some fall *to the* ground
Unsure how the rest go together,
  while *the* lost stay unfound
Maybe something could be built
  from what's left behind
If I can find somewhere
  to sort them sometime

I force the pieces in place
Now that I'm awoken
And I go back *to* sleep
Because everything's broken

Spiral

Wake   up
To the cold   and terror
To chills down the spine that remind the mind
Of the unrelenting spiral wherein nothing's fine

The   only   one who dares speak the truth...
A   monolithic   monologue of self-abuse...

The spiralling feedback, it never ends
Send me back into the yellowjackets again
Even if only for the burning stings
Send me back... just to feel something

Missing Pieces

How long do we hold on
Till we see that it's all gone?

A slightly worse version *of the* truth runs loose
Inspired by *a* memory' or *a* reoccurring dream
Uncertain what's fractured *or* what I've manufactured
What's calm as a **whisper** *tears through* like a **scream**

In my mind   I find I reassemble it still
It's filled with thrill-kills, *unsurprisingly, it spills*
Poisoned *by the* same toxic cycle *of* thoughts
Forging answers to questions I've **long since forgot**

We still hold on
Though it was lost all along

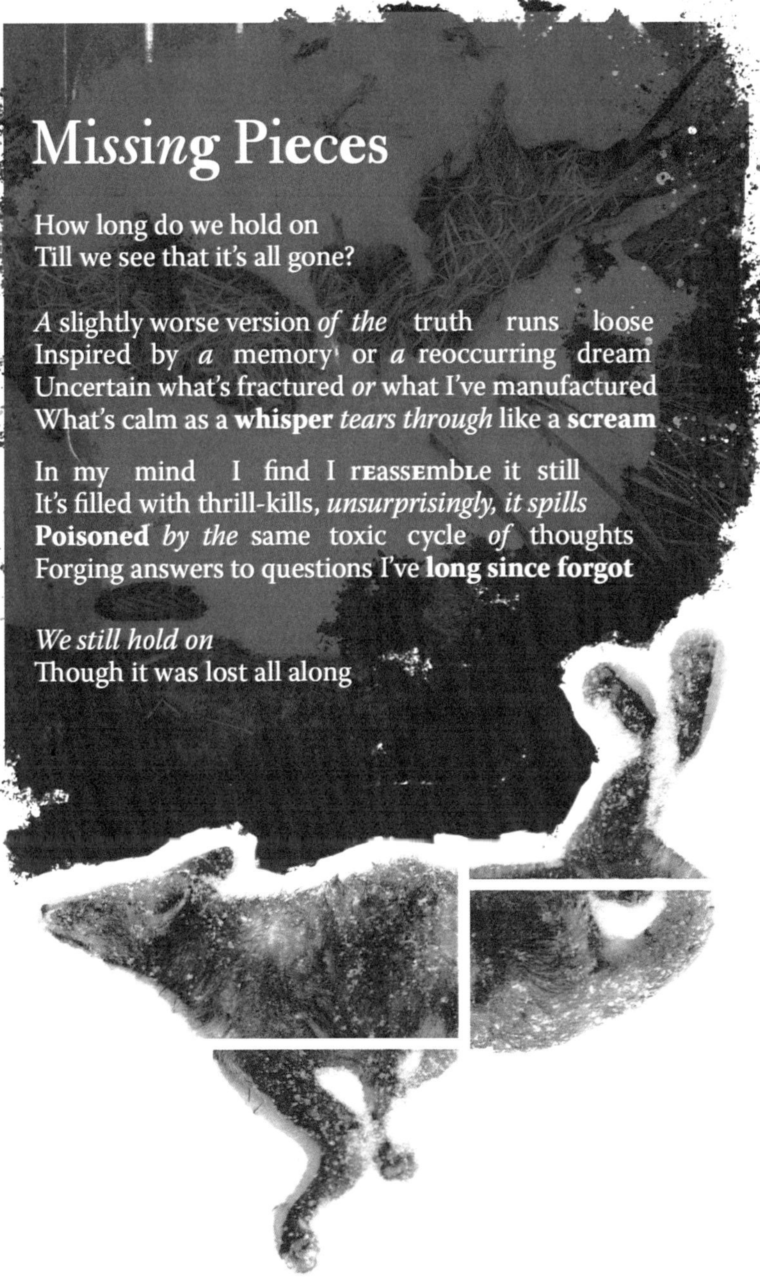

Last Days

Some days I just
want to disappear...
...in some ways I was
nevEr rEaLly here

From Monkey *to* Man *and* Back Again

A Life Less Lifeless

Slowly strangled through *years of neglect*
Dismissed *as* some demented reject
Now beaten, bleeding, torn apart
All that remains is this broken heart
Wrapped in **glass** and **rusty nails**
Over my shoulder an ANGEL wails
It sucks the wind out from my sails
And once again *defeat prevails*
So lay *to* waste this basket case
And erase this face from this lonely place
This useless man has been replaced
By the **wrath** *of the* **wraith** who's lost his faith
Surrounded in sorrow, just cancel tomorrow
Abandoned by hope, lean forward and choke
One last gasp in an off-key note
And **fade to black at the end of the rope**

106 Years Underwater
(OR: Echoes, Shadows, *and* Reflections)

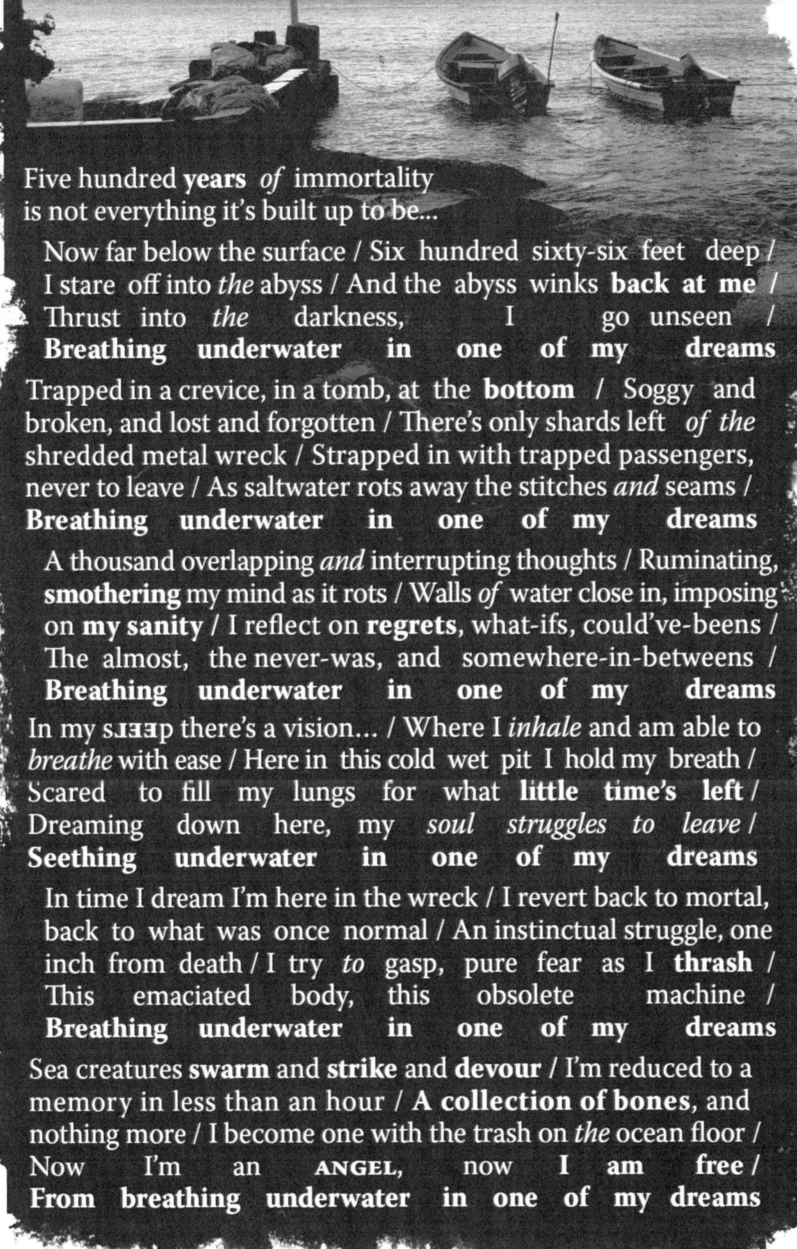

Five hundred **years** *of* immortality
is not everything it's built up to be...

Now far below the surface / Six hundred sixty-six feet deep /
I stare off into *the* abyss / And the abyss winks **back at me** /
Thrust into *the* darkness, I go unseen /
Breathing underwater in one of my dreams

Trapped in a crevice, in a tomb, at the **bottom** / Soggy and
broken, and lost and forgotten / There's only shards left *of the*
shredded metal wreck / Strapped in with trapped passengers,
never to leave / As saltwater rots away the stitches *and* seams /
Breathing underwater in one of my dreams

A thousand overlapping *and* interrupting thoughts / Ruminating,
smothering my mind as it rots / Walls *of* water close in, imposing
on **my sanity** / I reflect on **regrets**, what-ifs, could've-beens /
The almost, the never-was, and somewhere-in-betweens /
Breathing underwater in one of my dreams

In my sɹǝǝp there's a vision... / Where I *inhale* and am able to
breathe with ease / Here in this cold wet pit I hold my breath /
Scared to fill my lungs for what **little time's left** /
Dreaming down here, my *soul struggles to leave* /
Seething underwater in one of my dreams

In time I dream I'm here in the wreck / I revert back to mortal,
back to what was once normal / An instinctual struggle, one
inch from death / I try *to* gasp, pure fear as I **thrash** /
This emaciated body, this obsolete machine /
Breathing underwater in one of my dreams

Sea creatures **swarm** and **strike** and **devour** / I'm reduced to a
memory in less than an hour / **A collection of bones**, and
nothing more / I become one with the trash on *the* ocean floor /
Now I'm an ANGEL, now **I am free** /
From breathing underwater in one of my dreams

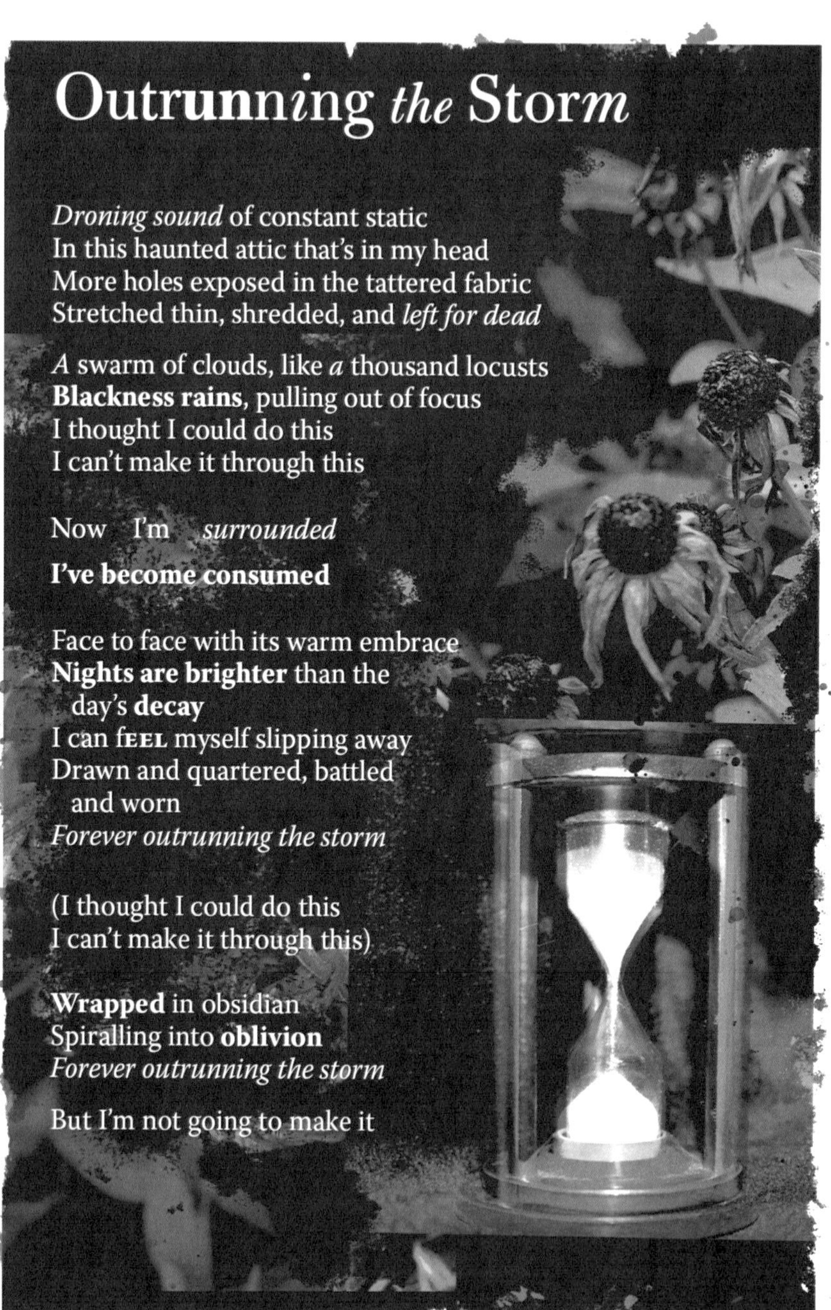

Outrunning *the* Storm

Droning sound of constant static
In this haunted attic that's in my head
More holes exposed in the tattered fabric
Stretched thin, shredded, and *left for dead*

A swarm of clouds, like *a* thousand locusts
Blackness rains, pulling out of focus
I thought I could do this
I can't make it through this

Now   I'm   *surrounded*

I've become consumed

Face to face with its warm embrace
Nights are brighter than the
  day's **decay**
I can FEEL myself slipping away
Drawn and quartered, battled
  and worn
Forever outrunning the storm

(I thought I could do this
I can't make it through this)

Wrapped in obsidian
Spiralling into **oblivion**
Forever outrunning the storm

But I'm not going to make it

Rabid Gød

†

Life tastes just like it should
In this landfill *of* **faith and hope**
Gnawing on my nagging tongue
And chase these daily pills with blood

Misanthropy is all we see
Hypocrisy *and* **these casualties**
Hearts begin to atrophy
And empathy is now deemed **weak**

It's funny how
It's better now
You're underground
Free to scream without *a* **sound**
Free to shout, Loud *as* your lungs allow
Your screams *and* **shouts are now drowned out**
Your empty words fall on deaf ears
Lies in disguise you've *spewed for years*

Through crooked teeth, you smile *and* nod
A new world waits through rusted gates
Fake your faith *and* face your fate
At the **feet** *of a* rabid god

†

Tangled *in the* Fishing Line

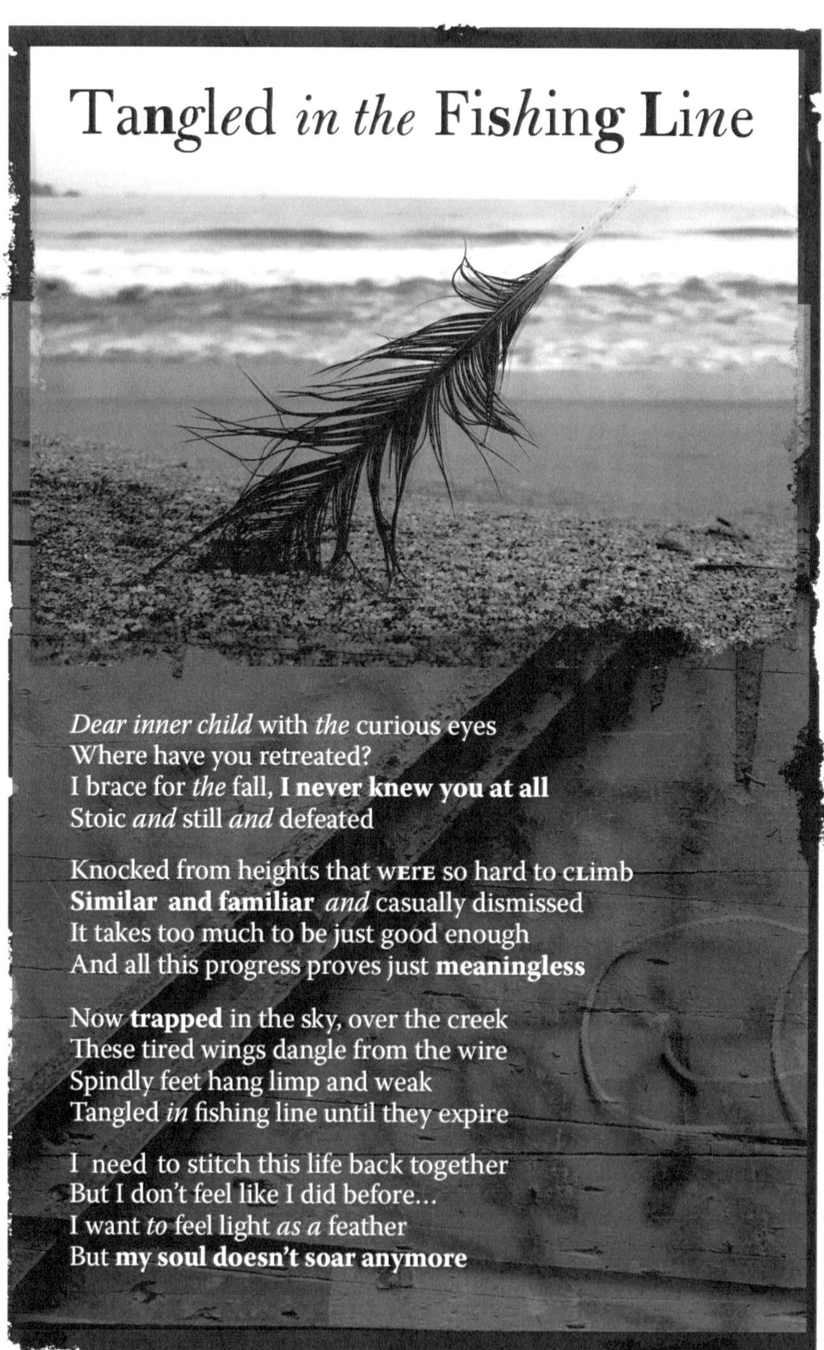

Dear inner child with *the* curious eyes
Where have you retreated?
I brace for *the* fall, **I never knew you at all**
Stoic *and* still *and* defeated

Knocked from heights that WERE so hard to CLImb
Similar and familiar *and* casually dismissed
It takes too much to be just good enough
And all this progress proves just **meaningless**

Now **trapped** in the sky, over the creek
These tired wings dangle from the wire
Spindly feet hang limp and weak
Tangled *in* fishing line until they expire

I need to stitch this life back together
But I don't feel like I did before…
I want *to* feel light *as a* feather
But **my soul doesn't soar anymore**

The **Dirty Demon King**

In my reoccurring dream I *am the* **Demon King**
Infected *by the* voices that only sing *in* screams
I drown *in the* frowns in this sea *of* useless clowns
And prick my fingers on this barbed wire crown

I am the Lord *of* Misery trampling *the* Garden *of* Eden
Sowing seeds *of* deception, waiting patiently *to* **reap them**
Servant *of the* **deviant, pulling strings behind** *the* curtain
I repent with *the* serpent, *and* lament *the* uncertain

The raspy voice *of* reason, ignoring all that you believe in
The Patronizing Saint, *the* heretic *and* **heathen**
Defiant and deceiving, **turning everything obscene**
I'm *the* dirty Demon King, *and* **I am all of these things**

The fantasy *and* **ecstasy**, *the* reality *and* **agony**
They all feel *the* same *to* me
I'm *in a* nightmare *in* this narcoleptic state
I don't want *to* **sleep**
Because
I
Dream
That
I'm
Awake

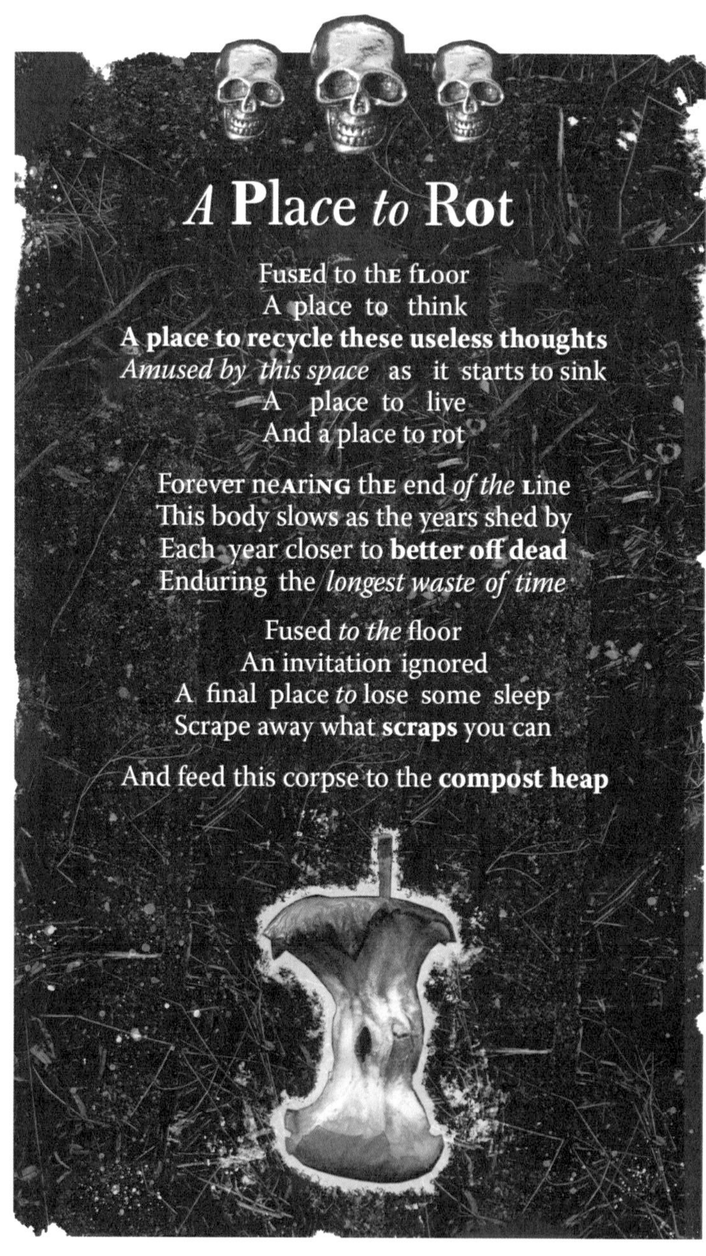

A **Place** *to* **Rot**

Fusᴇd to thᴇ fʟoor
A place to think
A place to recycle these useless thoughts
Amused by this space as it starts to sink
A place to live
And a place to rot

Forever neᴀriɴɢ thᴇ end *of the* ʟine
This body slows as the years shed by
Each year closer to **better off dead**
Enduring the *longest waste of time*

Fused *to the* floor
An invitation ignored
A final place *to* lose some sleep
Scrape away what **scraps** you can

And feed this corpse to the **compost heap**

Lucid Nightmare

Wake *to* **waste** another day
Watch   *the*   sun   rise
Watch   my   heart   **die**

Head down, I disappear into a world that isn't there
I can escape from this wasteland *of* disrepair
Head up, I see *the* **chaos that existed before**
So I put my head down *and* **disappear once more**
In a state *of* mind with my mind at stake
I await a fate that's running late
Dreams can die just by staying awake
So I face the day by wiping the slate
I neglect to reflect on *the* pain *of* penance
My absence far preferred over presence

But when *the* sun is done
No one knows just where I go
Become someone when the night's begun

Become nocturnal

Become   eternal

Lurking *in the* Dirt

The compANy I keep *is* keepinG mE from sLeep
In *the* dirt's where it lurks
It's whERE it crawLS *and* where it creeps
A long spindly shadow **reaches out to me**
Stretched across the ground, nipping at my feet

It follows me home

It won't let me go

And it swallows me whole

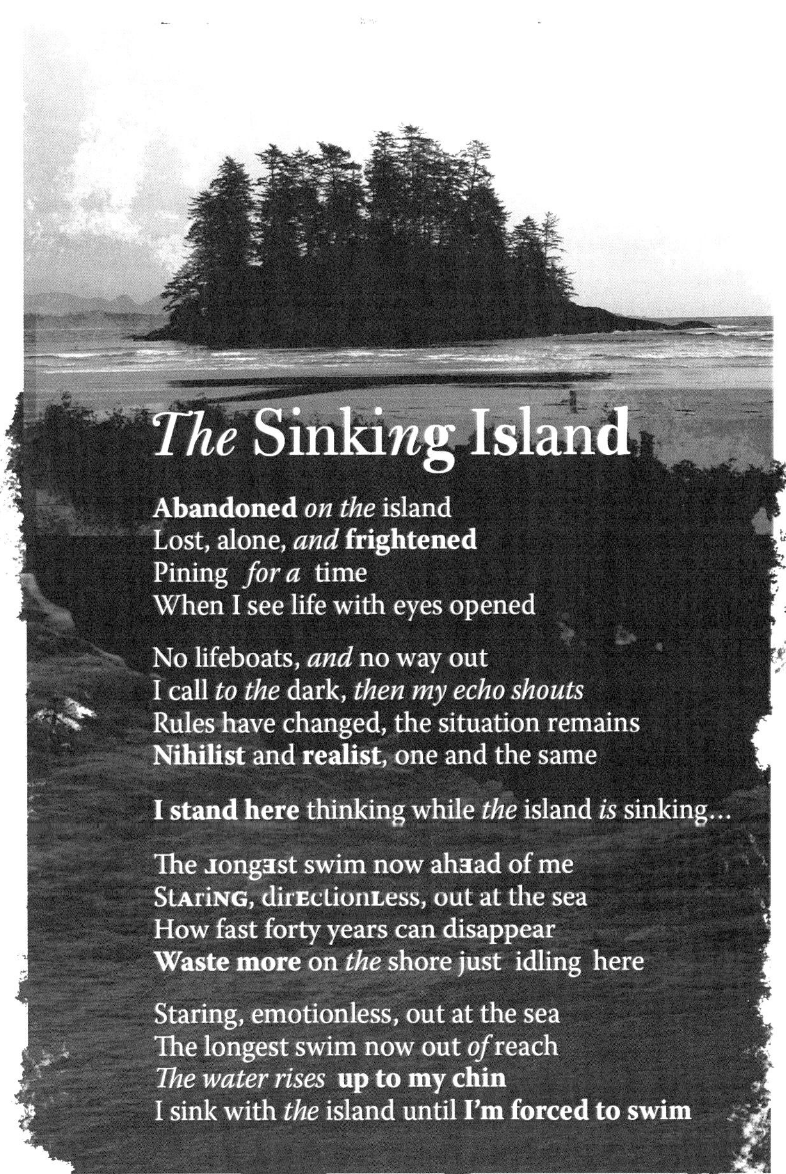

The Sinking Island

Abandoned *on the* island
Lost, alone, *and* **frightened**
Pining *for a* time
When I see life with eyes opened

No lifeboats, *and* no way out
I call *to the* dark, *then my echo shouts*
Rules have changed, the situation remains
Nihilist and **realist**, one and the same

I stand here thinking while *the* island *is* sinking…

The longest swim now ahead of me
Staring, directionless, out at the sea
How fast forty years can disappear
Waste more on *the* shore just idling here

Staring, emotionless, out at the sea
The longest swim now out *of* reach
The water rises **up to my chin**
I sink with *the* island until **I'm forced to swim**

Nothing *and* No One

Disappearing Act

I resent repentance *and* resist acceptance
As **demagogues** promise **demigods**
But deliver stray dogs and false idols
I become pseudocidal

This   illusion *of* hope
This   delusion *of* hope

Never *to* be seen *or* heard
Neither last word **nor whimper**
Without *a* sound, *falling further*
Disappearing into the ether...

Remission *from* Despair

These **tattered** things, these Icarus wings…
As *if* lured too far where *the* sirens sing
I'm drawn *to the* sun, *and* destined *to* fall
Another failure scratched *on* this prison wall

Another day where *the* darkness stays
Hope goes limp like *the* predator's prey
As **fair-weather friends** begin *to* rust
Seasons chANGE, *and* coLd **falls upon us**

Between dead leaves *and the* barren trees
The **dirt and grey** still have their place
The cold air hits, and the **summer's done**
But these beautiful days *are* more *than the sun*

Skin Prison

Involuntary solitude
Amplified *in* magnitude
Trapped inside myself
Until it all turns *numb*
New scars *to* wear
No bars *to* hold me
Just skin
Step in
See insidᴇ thᴇ ʟife sentence that's been given
All screams turn *silent* inside *the* **skin prison**

Leaves Line *the* Grave

Filthy cramped fingers sifting soil
Slaving a lifetime *to* **dig this hole**
No matter how deep *it* goes
Same as the first
Each fistful's just dirt

In all this time it's all I've made
Now dead leaves line the shallow grave
Lay my head down
And wait *for the* cold to come in waves

Each fistful's just dirt
Same as the first...

Thirst for the cure to this lifelong curse
No matter how bad it seems, it's so much worse
No heaven above, just this **hell on Earth**

Spitting Image

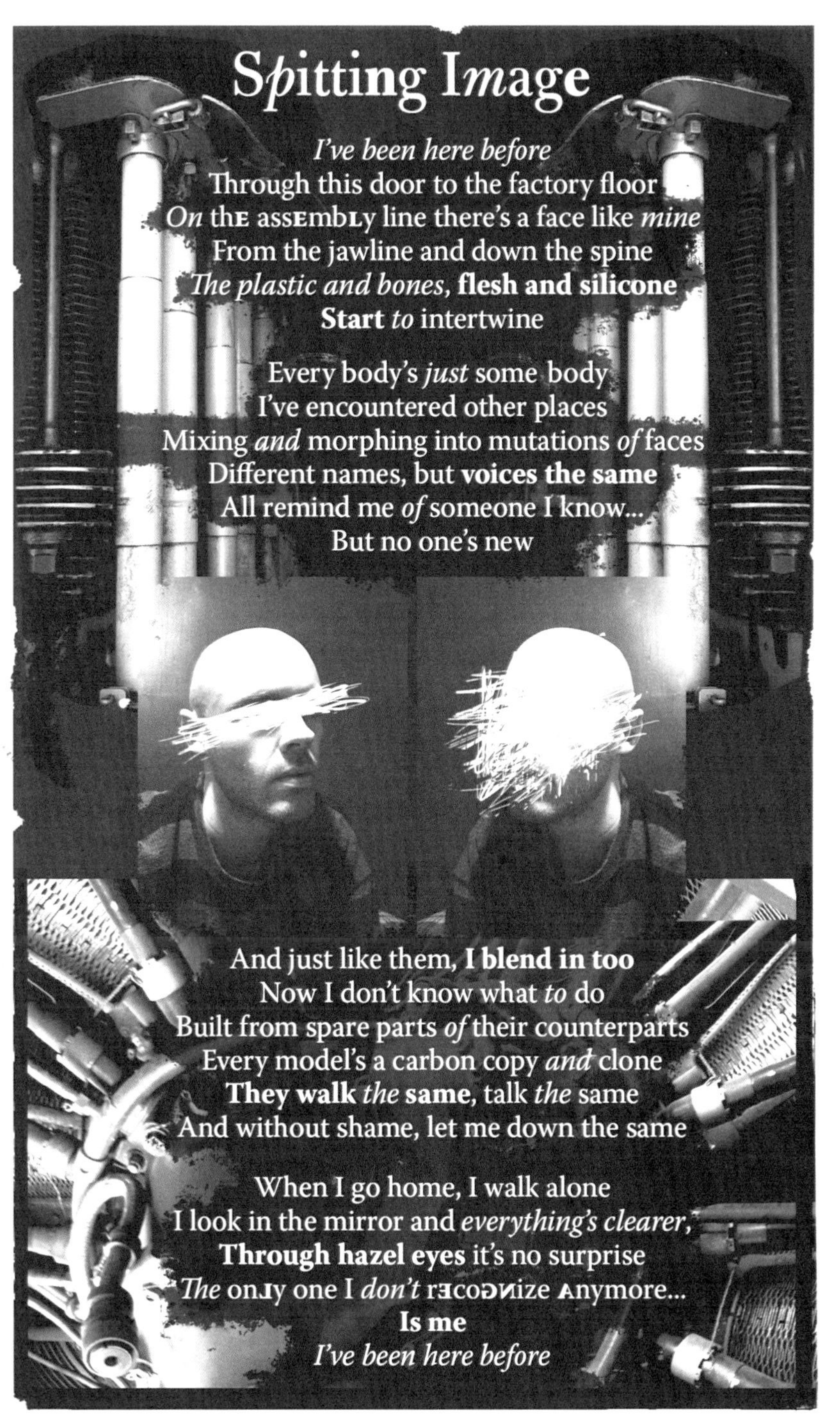

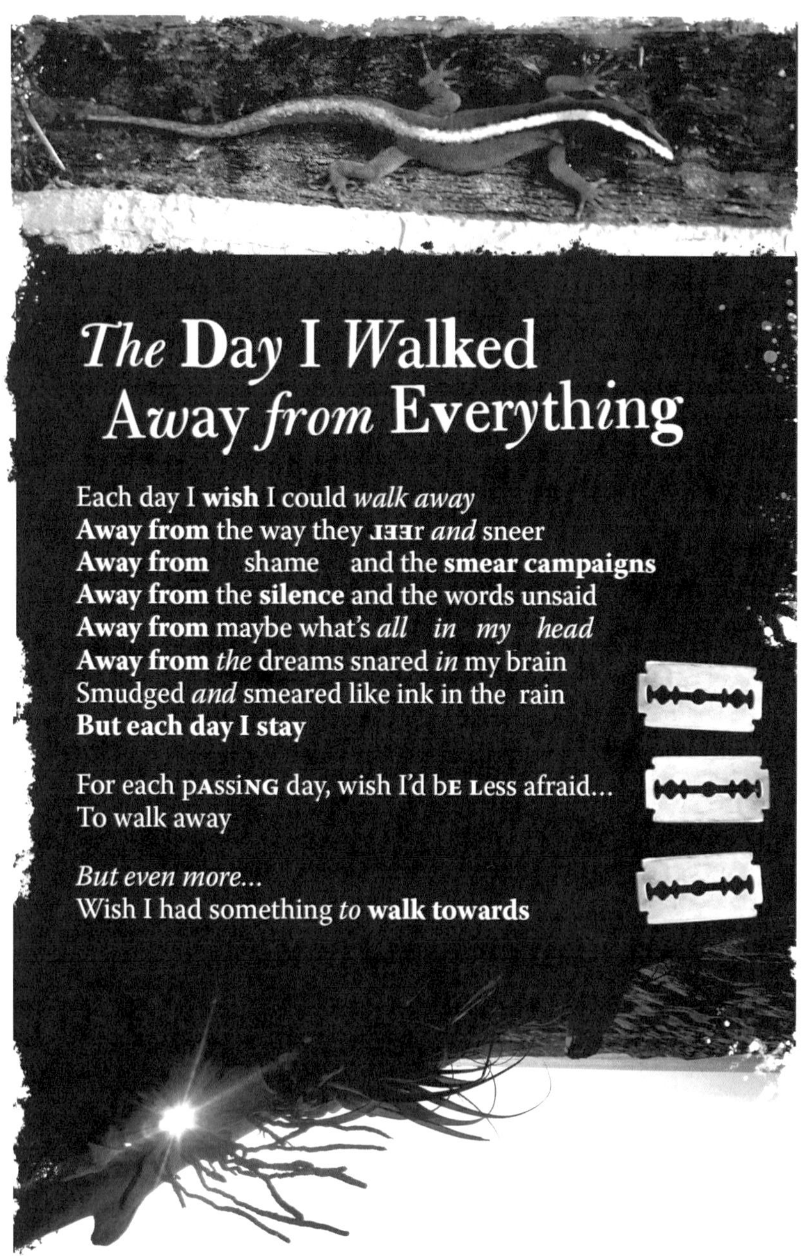

The **Day** I *Walked* Away *from* Everything

Each day I **wish** I could *walk away*
Away from the way they ʀᴇᴇʟ *and* sneer
Away from   shame   and the **smear campaigns**
Away from the **silence** and the words unsaid
Away from maybe what's *all   in   my   head*
Away from *the* dreams snared *in* my brain
Smudged *and* smeared like ink in the rain
But each day I stay

For each ᴘᴀssɪɴɢ day, wish I'd bᴇ ʟᴇss afraid...
To walk away

But even more...
Wish I had something *to* **walk towards**

Part II: Broken Wings

Angels & Eels

The most **beautiful souls** slur
  the words that they say
Friendly ears **turn deaf** as their
  smiles fade away
Frowns soon appear with **sharp
  teeth** *hid beneath*
Warm *and* kind twisted shapes
  in the face of disbelief

Trading feathers for gills
  and shedding their wings
Through pharyngeal jaws,
  none of them sing
Transformed and **deformed**,
  these wet, *slippery things*
It's hard *to* imagine
  what this could all mean

With *nothing to say,*
  and nothing to do
You're soon consumed
  in *the* **truth that looms**
While some *of* us rot
  and some of us bloom
You're **doomed** for gloom
  in *an* empty room

And it's finally revealed
  what's long been concealed
It's what *you suspected,*
  and deep down you feel
The **pretty** and the **ugly**,
  the **fake** and the **real**...
The ones that you trust
  are just **ANGEL**s *and* **EELS**

Dog Eat Dogma

Stranded somewhere between **apathy**
 and **anarchy**
The idea came to me with subtlety
 , and clarity
Then… all *of a* sudden *it* was all
 I could see
The blueprint *of* what I was
 destined *to be*

"A longtime coming clash
 with the icons
An ill-timed **spasm**
 of iconoclasm
A perverse burst *of*
 desperation prevails
In *a* message in a bottle
 of a Molotov cocktail"

 Faulty loyalty **breeds**
 swarms *of* **fleas**
The disease brings *the* masses
 to their *knees with ease*

"Roll over *and* **play dead**
Deep in sand, bury your head
Don't think twice, beg for your life
Heel, kneel, lie, cheat, and steal

Cut your teeth on the hand that feeds
Take more than you need while
 broken hearts bleed
Look the other way
 Speak when spoken to
 Sit, stay, obey"

The blueprint *of* what you are
 destined to do
You can't avoid it, not that you want to

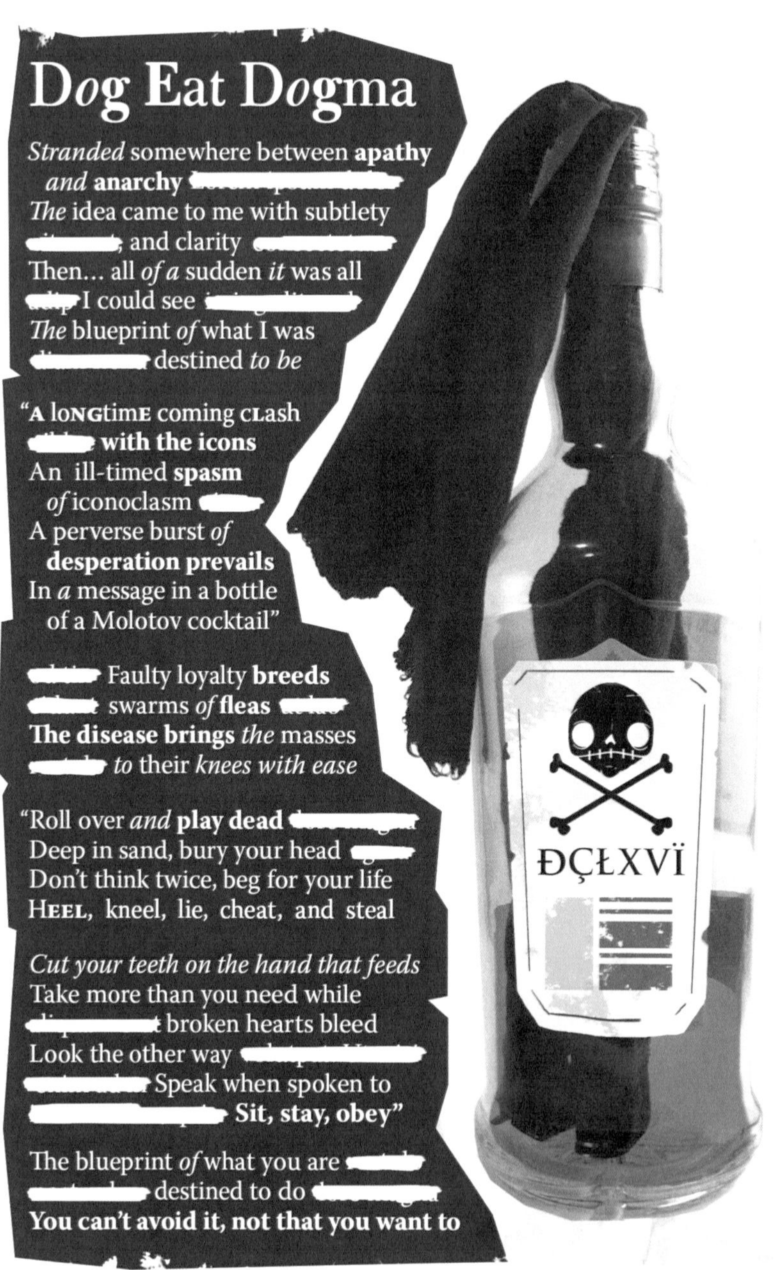

Just Rusty *and* Hollow

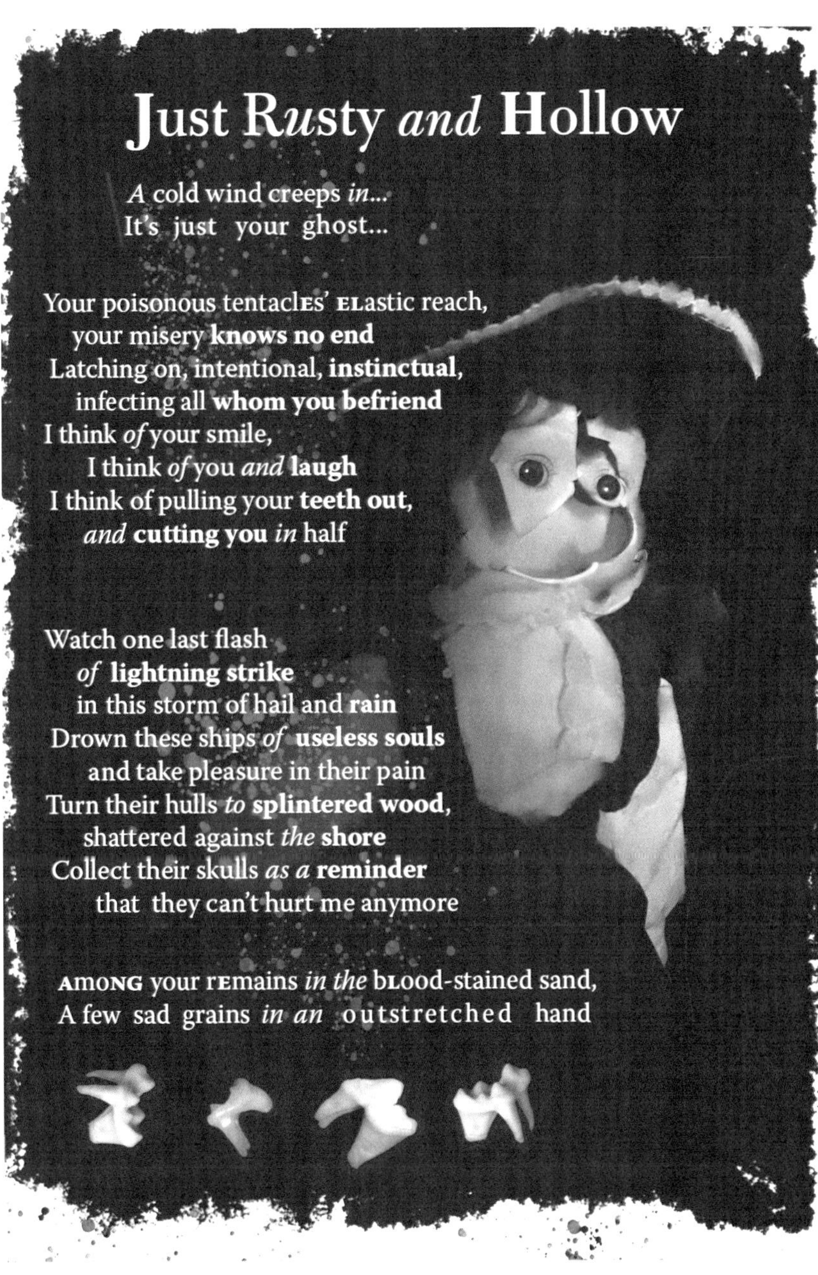

A cold wind creeps *in...*
It's just your ghost...

Your poisonous tentacles' elastic reach,
　your misery **knows no end**
Latching on, intentional, **instinctual**,
　infecting all **whom you befriend**
I think *of* your smile,
　I think *of* you *and* **laugh**
I think of pulling your **teeth out**,
　and **cutting you** *in* half

Watch one last flash
　of **lightning strike**
　in this storm of hail and **rain**
Drown these ships *of* **useless souls**
　and take pleasure in their pain
Turn their hulls *to* **splintered wood**,
　shattered against *the* **shore**
Collect their skulls *as a* **reminder**
　that they can't hurt me anymore

Among your remains *in the* blood-stained sand,
A few sad grains *in an* outstretched hand

Dea*d* En*d* La*b*yrinth

Hand *to* this cold stone wall
Navig**ATING** th**E** **L**abyrinth
You haunt my peripherals
        with your **absence**

You claim you're there
But for **E**ach lon**ELY** step on this long path
There's no laughter *in the air*

    Through *the* hole I fall
    Into *the* **empty dungeon** I land
    On bludgeoned *and* bloody hands

        The bones crack like thunder
        If I ever get through
            it remains unknown *to* you
        If I'm lost down here,
            you'll **never** wonder

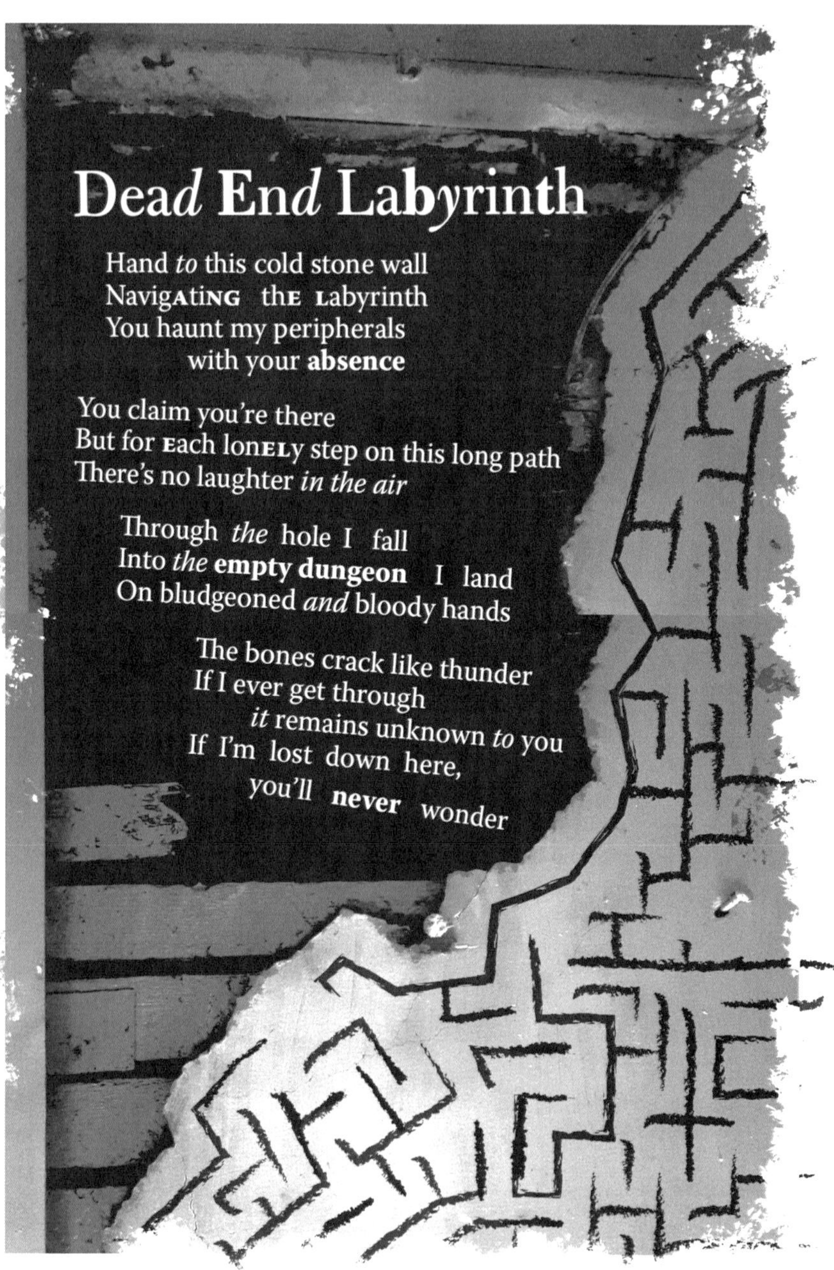

Poison Arrow

Archer's *poison arrow* arcs through arteries
Bruised lover's **broken heart** takes cover
Another misstep in thᴇ ʟong grass
Sidestepping the   bear traps
Grip the handle, greet *the* blade of the knife
Twisted in the meat *of the* back half of my life

I beat and breathe life into you, there on the floor
I resuscitate you only to suffocate you once more
Cᴀst into the ɴothinɢɴᴇss where you beʟong
And somehow, **still**, this *life goes on*

Your
soulless
insincerity
inspires
intolerance
in
me

In *a* Cardboard House

In *a* cardboard house for two
Play all day,
Just him *and* you

EVERY day's the same, up in fLames
It's what you always knew
Black clouds abound, *and* rain comes down
Four walls warp around you, *it comes unglued*

Nothing new,
Just him and you
In *a* cardboard house for two

End *of the* Emptiness

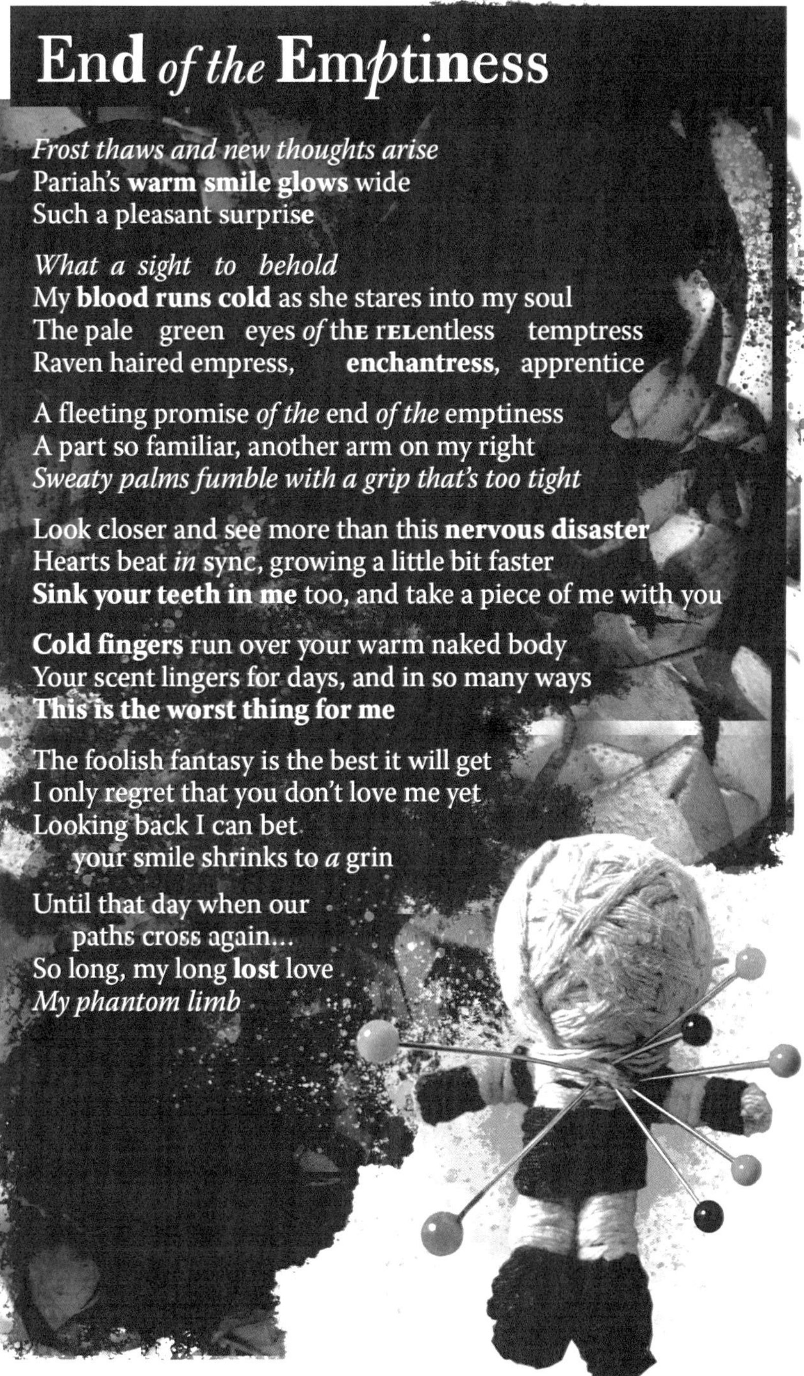

Frost thaws and new thoughts arise
Pariah's **warm smile glows** wide
Such a pleasant surprise

What a sight   to   behold
My **blood runs cold** as she stares into my soul
The pale   green   eyes *of* the relentless   temptress
Raven haired empress,   **enchantress**,   apprentice

A fleeting promise *of the* end *of the* emptiness
A part so familiar, another arm on my right
Sweaty palms fumble with a grip that's too tight

Look closer and see more than this **nervous disaster**
Hearts beat *in* sync, growing a little bit faster
Sink your teeth in me too, and take a piece of me with you

Cold fingers run over your warm naked body
Your scent lingers for days, and in so many ways
This is the worst thing for me

The foolish fantasy is the best it will get
I only regret that you don't love me yet
Looking back I can bet
    your smile shrinks to *a* grin

Until that day when our
    paths cross again…
So long, my long **lost** love
My phantom limb

Clawing *at a* Door *that* Will Never O**p**en

Open wide,
And fall inside these arms,
Wide open

Falling for these lies,
Fallen apart,
Now **blamed** *for* falling

Crawling *in the* dark,
In the deep,
There's no shame *in* crawling

Sleep now...
The escape *is* temporary...
Now **sleep**

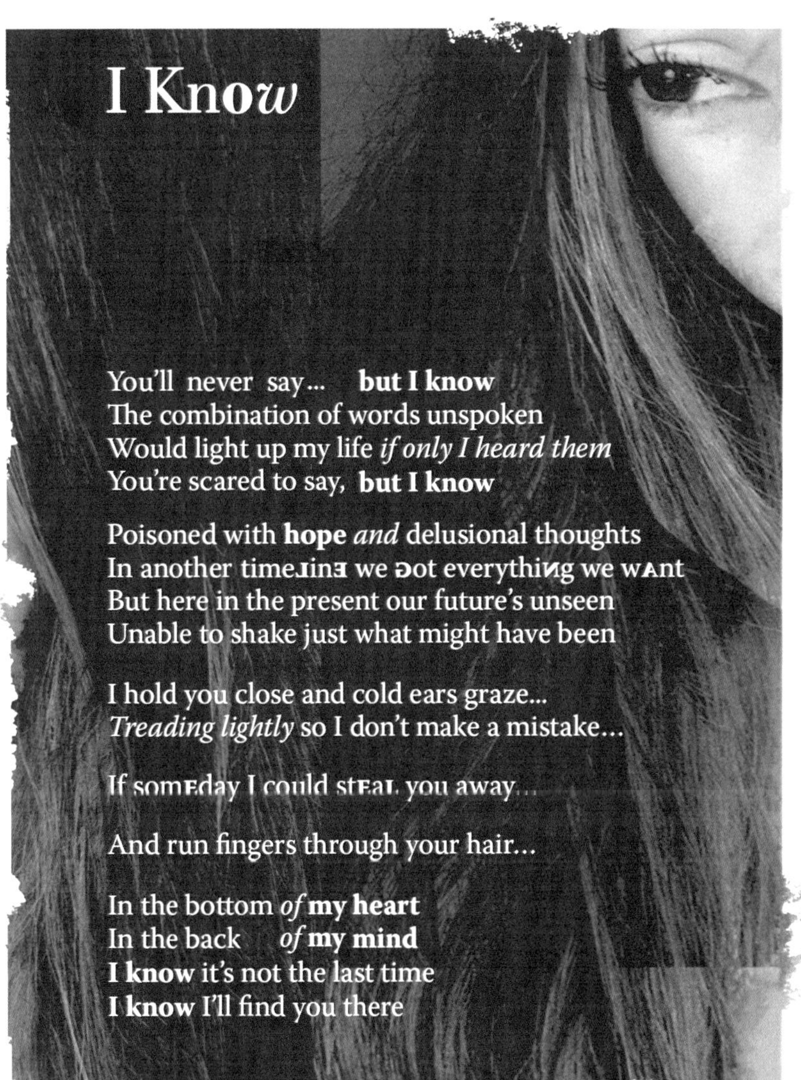

I Know

You'll never say... **but I know**
The combination of words unspoken
Would light up my life *if only I heard them*
You're scared to say, **but I know**

Poisoned with **hope** *and* delusional thoughts
In another timeline we got everything we want
But here in the present our future's unseen
Unable to shake just what might have been

I hold you close and cold ears graze...
Treading lightly so I don't make a mistake...

If someday I could steal you away...

And run fingers through your hair...

In the bottom *of* **my heart**
In the back *of* **my mind**
I know it's not the last time
I know I'll find you there

Falling Down *the* Stairs

See your scraped *and* bloody face
Staring up from the hardwood floor
Stumbled down *the* **spiral staircase**
You say it's enough, *but you need more...*

But you don't know what for

You push yourself, just like before
Like a rag doll off the shelf
A crumpled mess splayed on the floor
All warning signs go ignored...

But you don't know what for

Broken neck *and* **twisted limbs**
You climb back up *then you do it again*
Shattered heart *and* **body parts**
You lie there scattered *in* disrepair...

But now I just don't care

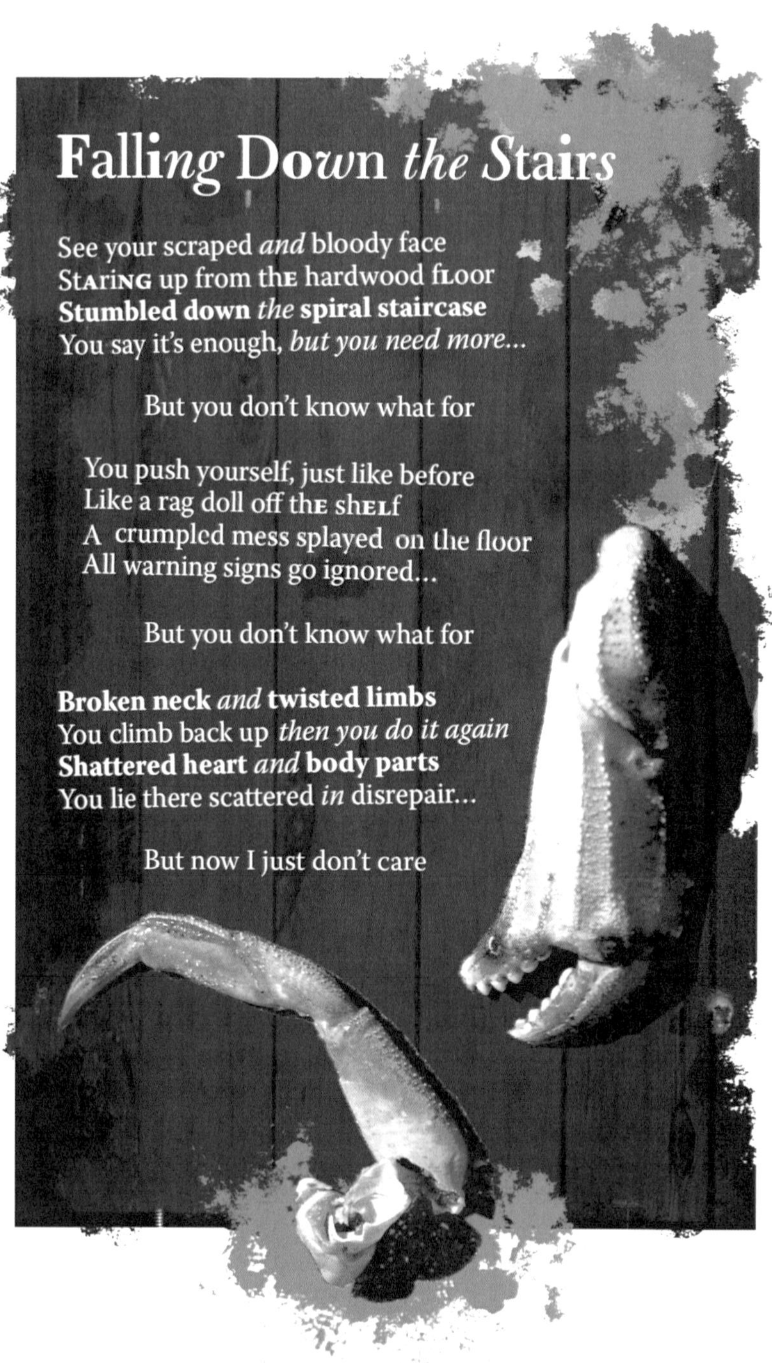

Scars *and* Stripes

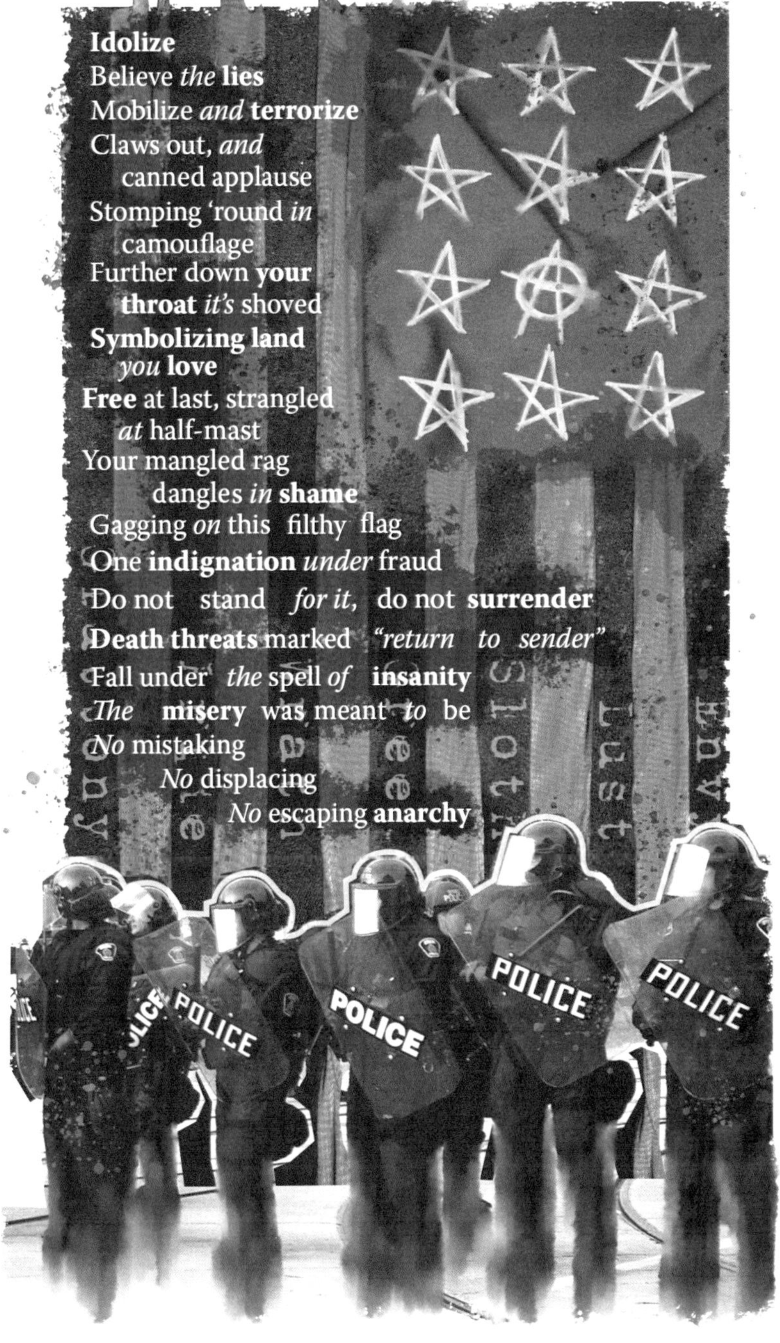

Ghost Ships *in the* Mist

Breathe in, my ANGEL *in exile...*
It's bEEn *a* whiLe
Soles *are* wearing thin, dogs *are* closing in
Teeth are sinking in, deep into your skin

A **new dawn** begins, where...
The air is thick with a **blitzkrieg** *of* **prayer**
There's no one there *and* no one cares

Loose ends pulled that come undone
Reveal one thing still believed by some

That one day *everything will be okay*

But every day in every way
You're deceived by every
                    word they say
This hopeless loneliness
                    never fades
As the days give way
            it comes in spades

From the bottom rung, a requiem,
The stray heart's song that's left unsung
Ash rains down and lands on our tongues
It fills our mouths, our time has come

There's fire *in* your heart

Exhale the smoke in your lungs

13 Minutes

Inked arms and goth ANGEL charm
Black paisley knotted across your hair
There you appear, *descending the stairs...*
Too good to be true, this old *pain* FEELS *new*
We wait at the gates, relieved our friends run late
Sucked in by a smile that shines for miles
Throttled by your laugh *and* I'm **gladly strangled**
I introduce myself and so do you
You hang on each word, and I do too
I tell myself that you're not real
And other things I refuse to feel
I find myself in denial for good reason
I tell myself lies I claim to believe in
My thoughts are blurry, **shrouded in mist**
I do my best and try to resist...

Women like you don't really exist

Mirrored circles hide your eyes
I look away when I start to despise
The **reflected fool**
Who proves delusional
Who insists on conjuring
an imaginary world
Where he's built *a* life
with this mystery girl
But this won't last
Thirteen minutes burns fast
And just like that, it's come and passed
And before long you're gone
But in that short time *you prove me wrong*
There's women like you somewhere out there too
But the truth remains: there's only one **you**
The vision of our life lingers long in my head
And I'm **left to love** this *memory instead*

Safe from summer sun, tucked *in the* shade
I'll wait by the gates, just in case...
Just in case you come back one day
The fastest friend I've ever made

Ka Nani Loa

Racing, *faster*
Outrunning **disaster**
Falling *and* breaking
Defeated,   receding

I can hear your heart

Now you can't stand
The way *the* **world rips through**
Its clawed grip slips into you
And **strips you   down**

Take my hand till you can stand again
Link those fingers with mine,
   and look in my eyes
BeɹiɘvƎ me,   it's true
Believe me when I tell you

Someday you'll see you as I do:
Someone's who's bulletproof
You'll stray with the wounds from your   worst days
Away *to the* **warmest place** where your heart plays

I can see it now...

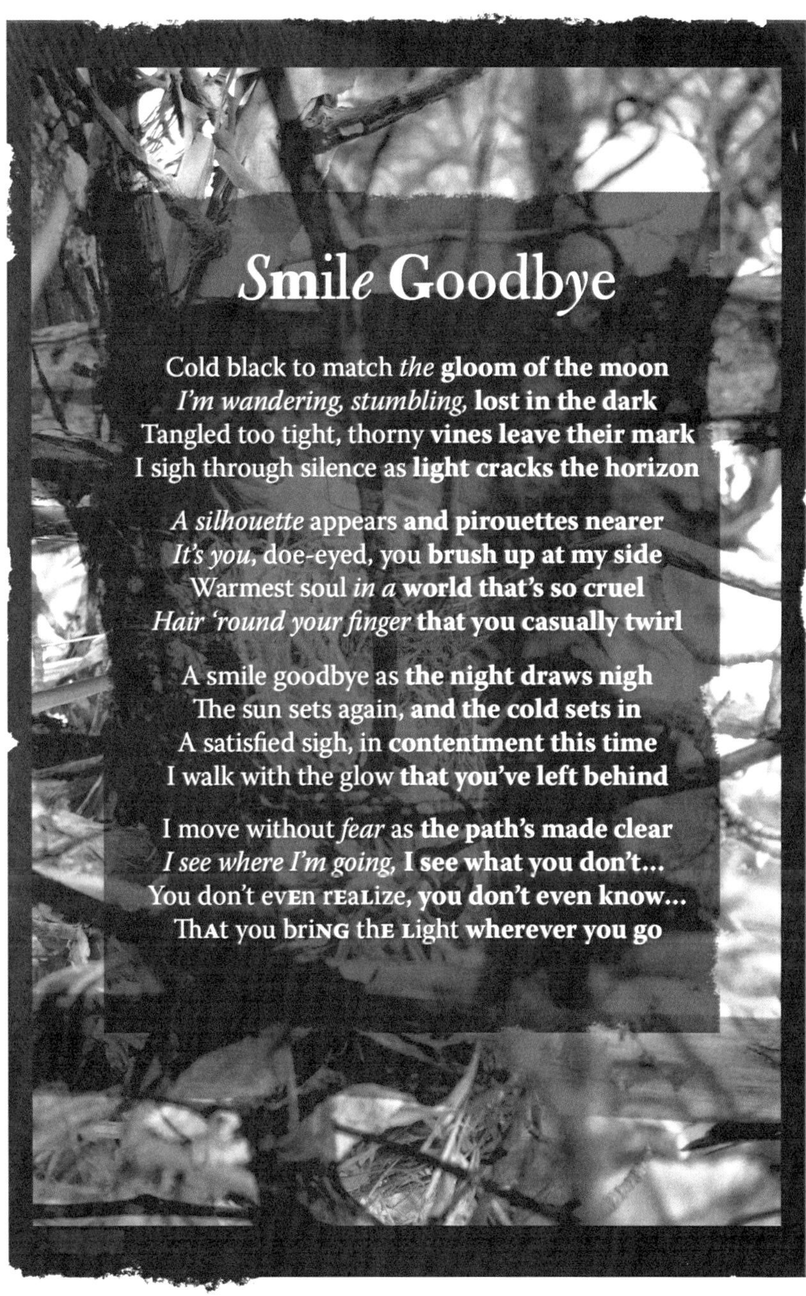

Smile Goodbye

Cold black to match *the* **gloom of the moon**
I'm wandering, stumbling, **lost in the dark**
Tangled too tight, thorny **vines leave their mark**
I sigh through silence as **light cracks the horizon**

A silhouette appears **and pirouettes nearer**
It's you, doe-eyed, you **brush up at my side**
Warmest soul *in a* **world that's so cruel**
Hair 'round your finger **that you casually twirl**

A smile goodbye as **the night draws nigh**
The sun sets again, **and the cold sets in**
A satisfied sigh, in **contentment this time**
I walk with the glow **that you've left behind**

I move without *fear* as **the path's made clear**
I see where I'm going, **I see what you don't...**
You don't even realize, **you don't even know...**
That you bring the light **wherever you go**

Where th**E** **E**ntrai**L**s lead, *the* **creature** feeds
Its **demon seed** sewn among *the weeds*
Run *and* hide *and* **catch your breath**
Look behind to find there's no one left
Your biggest fear *is* that *you'll disappear*
It hears this fear throughout *the* year
In *darkest days* of **panic** *and* relief
Real as it seems, *the* creature's make believe...

Pretty Ugly

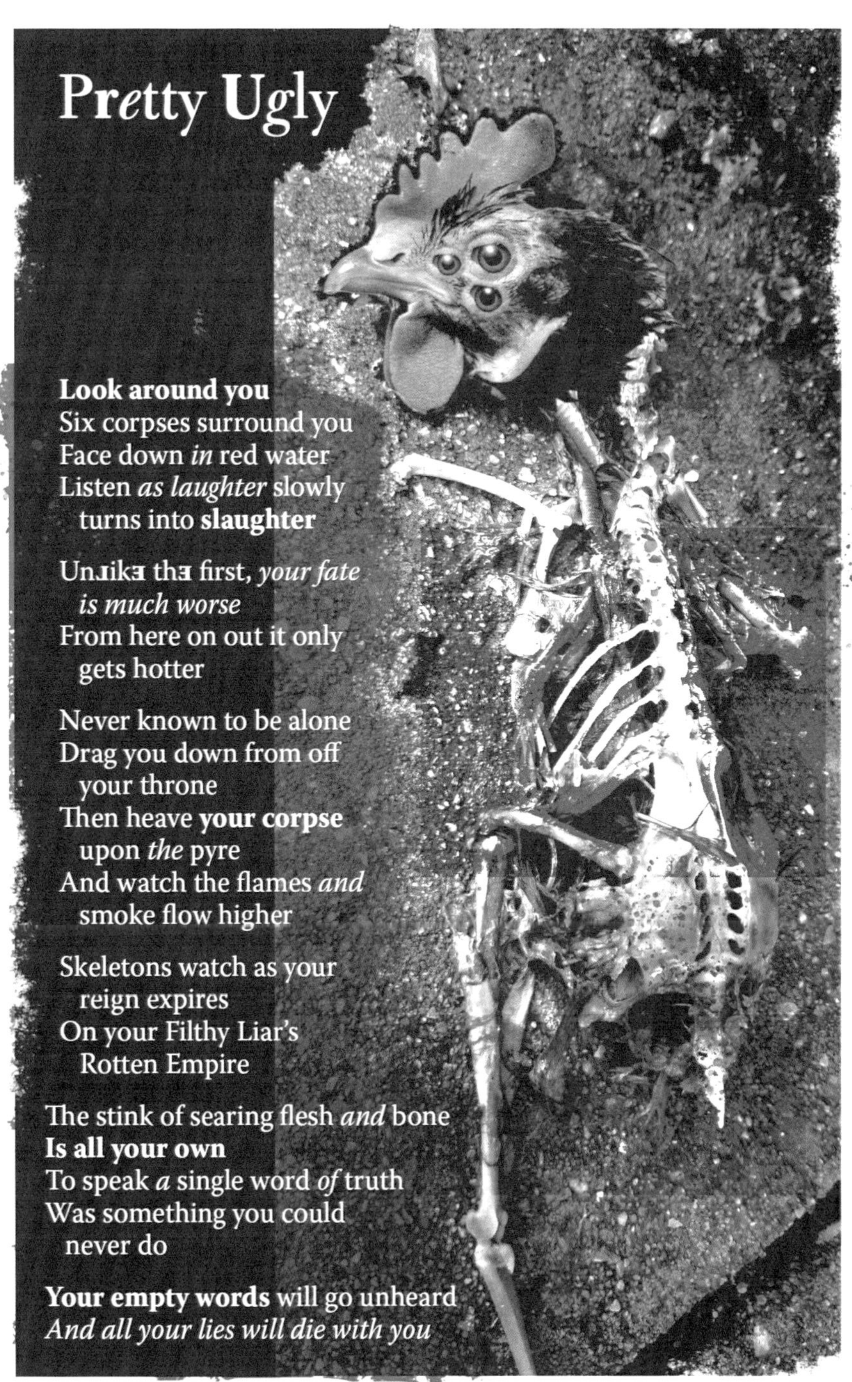

Look around you
Six corpses surround you
Face down *in* red water
Listen *as laughter* slowly
   turns into **slaughter**

Unlike the first, *your fate
is much worse*
From here on out it only
   gets hotter

Never known to be alone
Drag you down from off
   your throne
Then heave **your corpse**
   upon *the* pyre
And watch the flames *and*
   smoke flow higher

Skeletons watch as your
   reign expires
On your Filthy Liar's
   Rotten Empire

The stink of searing flesh *and* bone
Is all your own
To speak *a* single word *of* truth
Was something you could
   never do

Your empty words will go unheard
And all your lies will die with you

Scathen

The winding path she stumbles over only **slows her down**
The winding river next to her **beckons her to drown**
Second guesses, *and* secondhand dresses, unhemmed
She's not living *in the* shadows, she's dying in them
She's screamed *and* cried out her lungs and eyes
While an unwise voice in her head slurs lies
She could save HERSELf *if* she could break away
But her soul's sucked dry each day she tries

Another loss each time she dares to play
Because no one here gets out **unscathed**

Lessons unlearned, all mistakes remade
They **never** looked her way
Never learned her name
She reinvents herself but reverts *to the* same
She dreams to drain the **nightmare** from her brain
And numb *the* pain that *throbs in her head*
She dreams to **die in her sleep** each night
But she **wakes up alive** instead

Athazagoraphobia

Take heed, child
Go forth, **but be forewarned**
You were not raised to be feral
Your days are devoid of pity or praise
And now you face peril
Staring down the barrel
Of the petty fetid filth *of* this world

Life is coarse *and* remorseless
It will violate you
It will vandalize *and* invalidate you
Disappoint *and* dehumanize you
Deceive you *and* euthanize you
Denigrate... emasculate... suffocate
Regret
Forget
And humiliate you
Attempt to snuff you when
　　　it's had enough *of* you
Debase *and* deface, and bend and break you
Strangle *and* **mangle,** and brutalize you
Berate *and* hate, and **neutralize** you
Cripple you and cackle
　　　as the sadness ripples out from you
Infect, neglect, *and* disrespect you
Beat, *and* breed, *and* then defeat you
Refuse *and* confuse
Misuse
Abuse
And fucking destroy you

Life will deconstruct and then rebuild you
In a desecrated, manipulated image
Mutilated
Mutated
And reborn anew
Take heed, child
There's nothing you can do

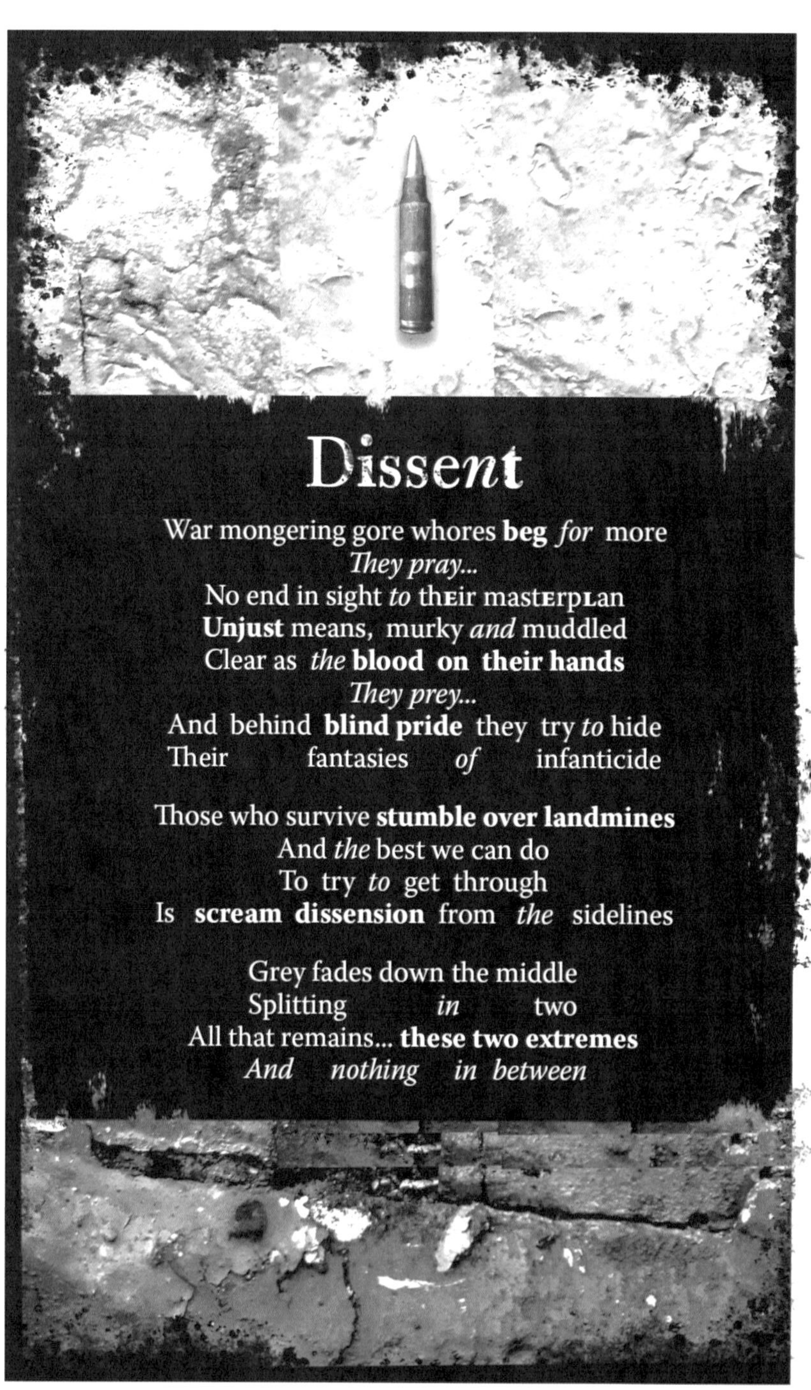

Dissent

War mongering gore whores **beg** *for* more
They pray...
No end in sight *to* thɛir masterplan
Unjust means, murky *and* muddled
Clear as *the* **blood on their hands**
They prey...
And behind **blind pride** they try *to* hide
Their   fantasies   *of*   infanticide

Those who survive **stumble over landmines**
And *the* best we can do
To try *to* get through
Is **scream dissension** from *the* sidelines

Grey fades down the middle
Splitting   *in*   two
All that remains... **these two extremes**
And   nothing   in between

Collapse of the Ringmaster's Dirty Circus

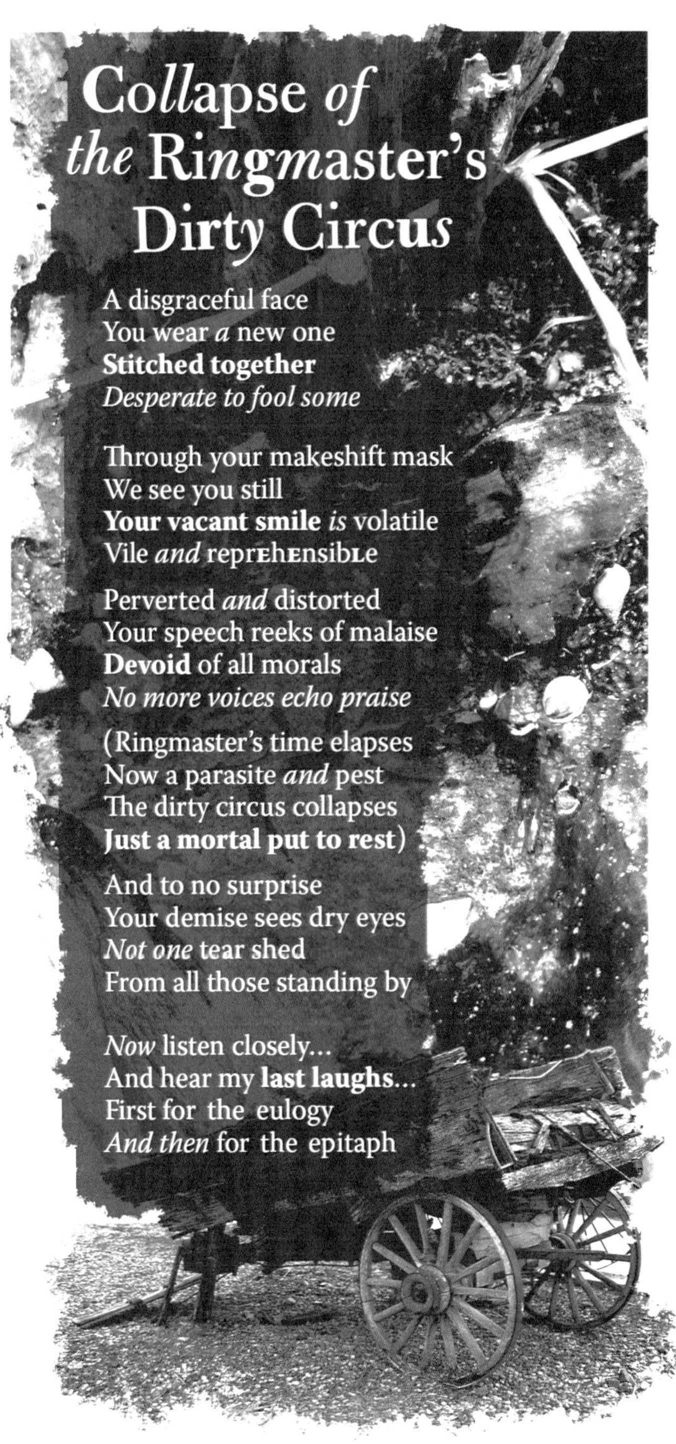

A disgraceful face
You wear *a* new one
Stitched together
Desperate to fool some

Through your makeshift mask
We see you still
Your vacant smile *is* volatile
Vile *and* reprehensible

Perverted *and* distorted
Your speech reeks of malaise
Devoid of all morals
No more voices echo praise

(Ringmaster's time elapses
Now a parasite *and* pest
The dirty circus collapses
Just a mortal put to rest)

And to no surprise
Your demise sees dry eyes
Not one tear shed
From all those standing by

Now listen closely…
And hear my **last laughs**…
First for the eulogy
And then for the epitaph

The Red Lamp

On some starry night
With or without the moon
Through *the* **crashing waves**
I'll crawl back to you
Across **ocean** *and* **sand**
Where this anchored heart lands
And meet you under *the* light *of the* red lamp again...

Snowprints

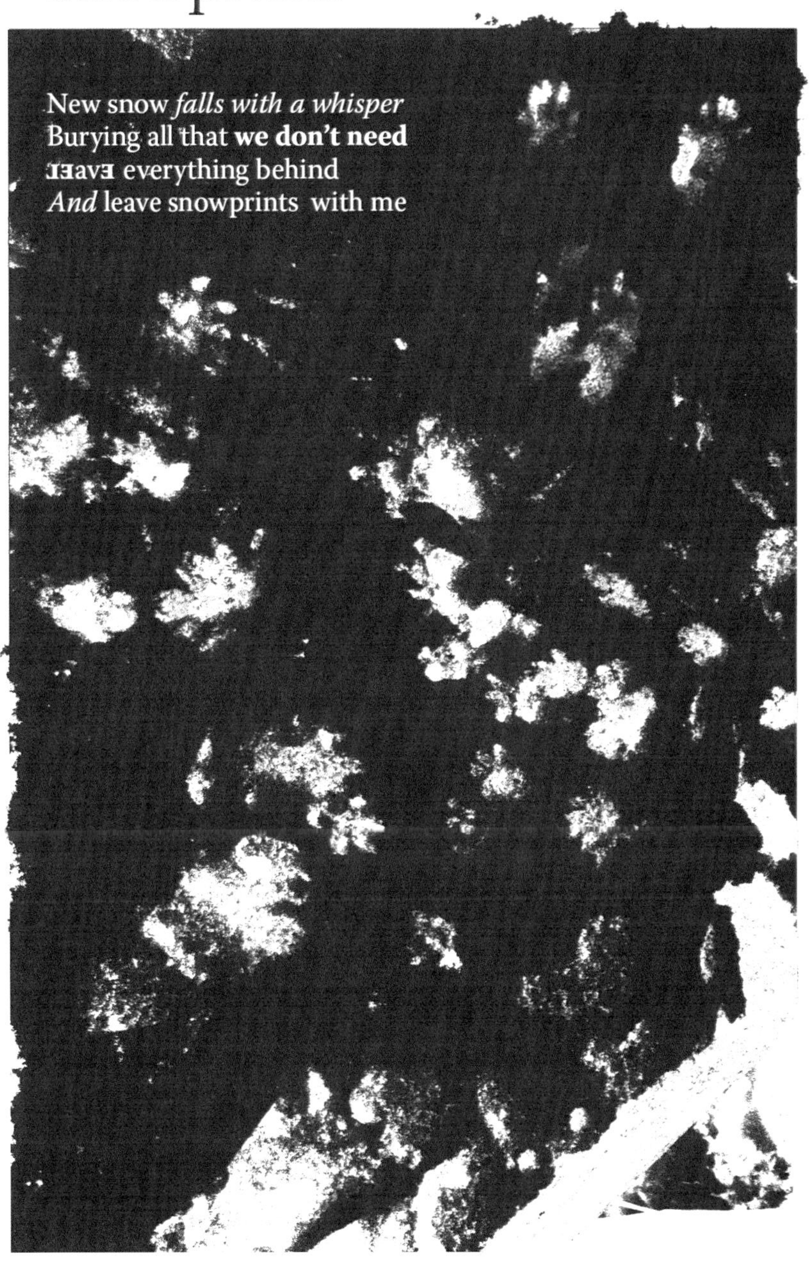

New snow *falls with a whisper*
Burying all that **we don't need**
Leave everything behind
And leave snowprints with me

Arsenic *for the* Effort

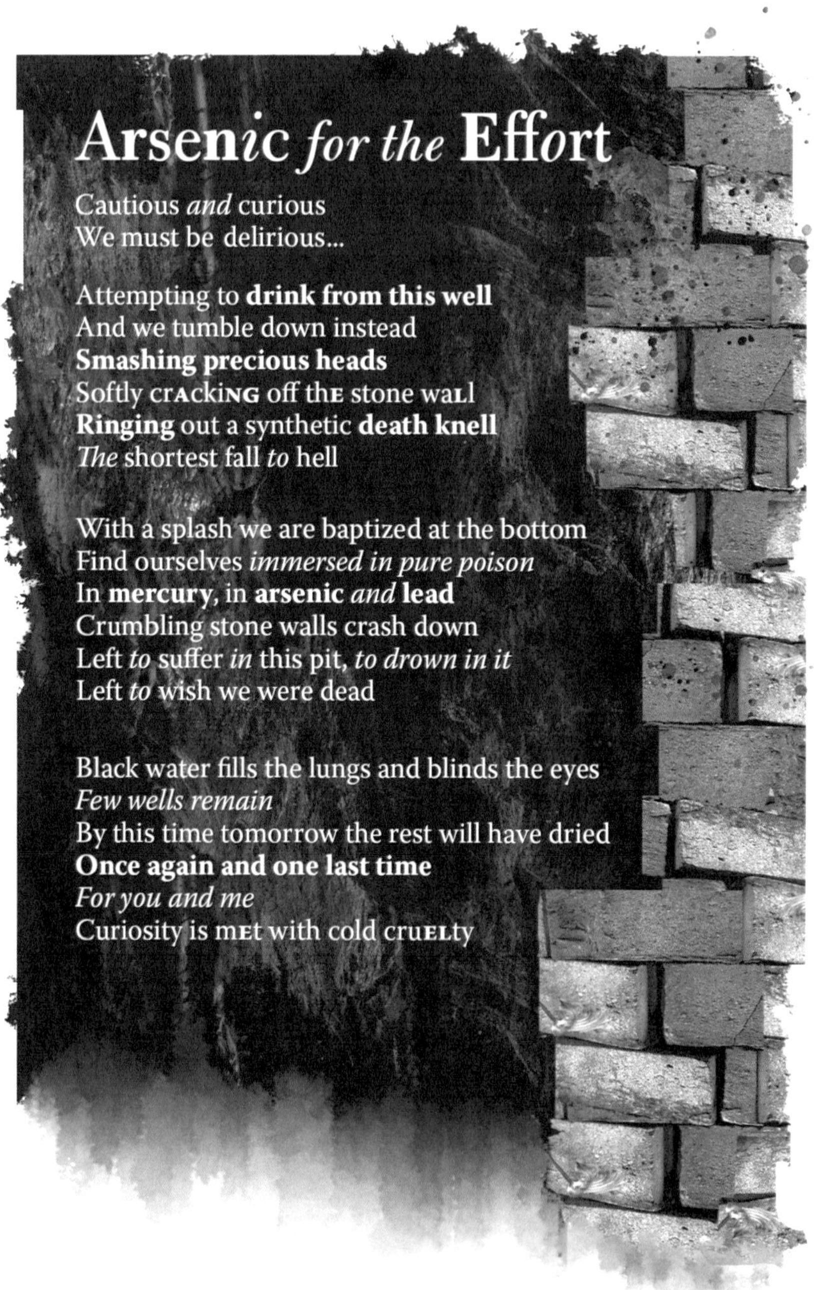

Cautious *and* curious
We must be delirious...

Attempting to **drink from this well**
And we tumble down instead
Smashing precious heads
Softly cracking off the stone wall
Ringing out a synthetic **death knell**
The shortest fall *to* hell

With a splash we are baptized at the bottom
Find ourselves *immersed in pure poison*
In **mercury**, in **arsenic** *and* **lead**
Crumbling stone walls crash down
Left *to* suffer *in* this pit, *to drown in it*
Left *to* wish we were dead

Black water fills the lungs and blinds the eyes
Few wells remain
By this time tomorrow the rest will have dried
Once again and one last time
For you and me
Curiosity is met with cold cruelty

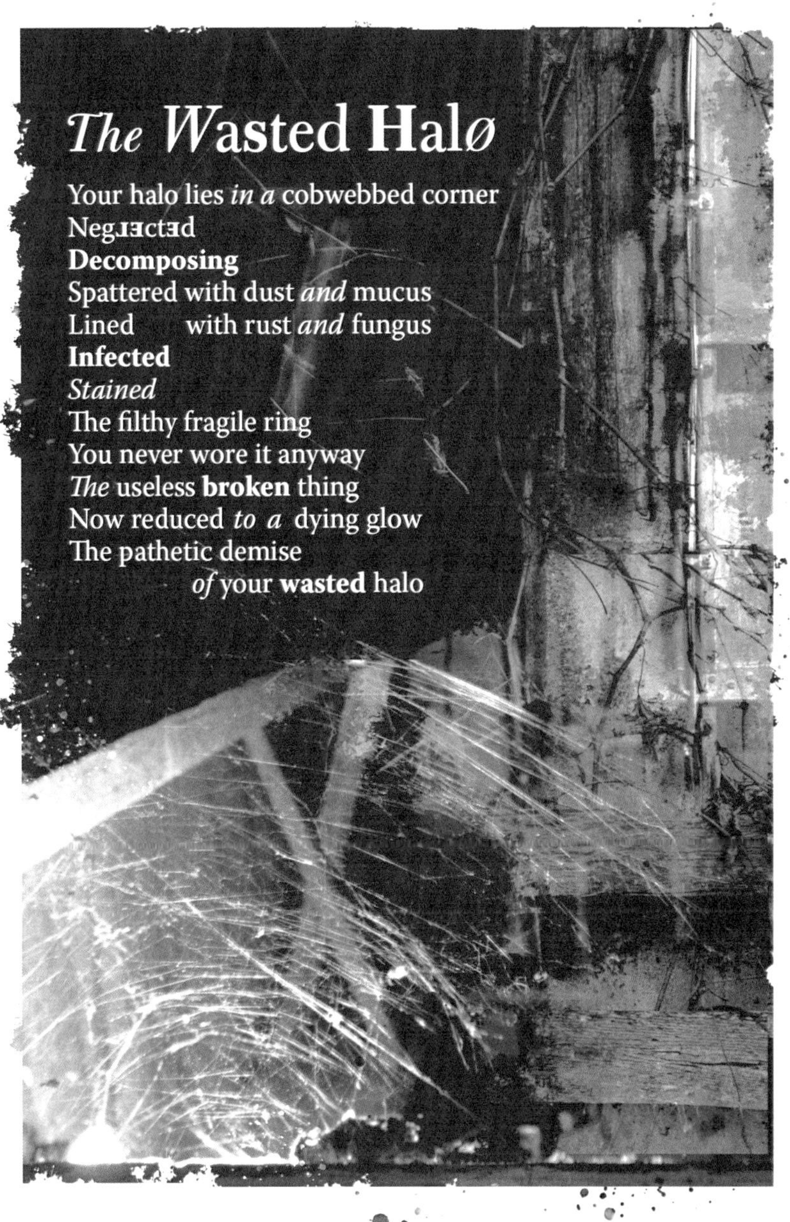

The Wasted **Halø**

Your halo lies *in a* cobwebbed corner
Neglected
Decomposing
Spattered with dust *and* mucus
Lined   with rust *and* fungus
Infected
Stained
The filthy fragile ring
You never wore it anyway
The useless **broken** thing
Now reduced *to a* dying glow
The pathetic demise
          of your **wasted** halo

Wherever You Are

Good morning, friend
Wake up again
To skies awash with **black** *and* **grey**
Another dreary day awaits

The usual *pains strain hearts* and then
Tears stain EYES LIKE **rain with no end**

But I awake *to the* same
And it's *a* beautiful day
Because you woke up too
Good morning, friend

   Pitch Black Heart Syndrome

 Pitch Black Heart Syndrome